Dancing
with Death

By Celeste Rose

A deep-felt lament of grief and recovery, beautiful and powerful.

Allyson Jean Bennett

Red Moons Press
Presents

Dancing with Death

A True Testament to Grief and Recovery

By CELESTE ROSE
&
ALLYSON JEAN BENNETT

The unexpected death of Ms. Rose's twenty-seven year old daughter hits family and friends like a San Francisco earthquake. They bend together to pick up unexplained pieces of Allyson's life and try to make some sense of her death.

To Robin
From Aunt Celeste
with full love
Nov. 2012

© 2012 by Celeste Rose

All characters appearing in this work are factual. Some names have been changed to protect the privacy of the individuals.

The final approval of this literary material is granted by the author.

First Printing

A RED MOONS PRESS PUBLICATION

ISBN-13: 978-0-9847324-7-0
ISBN-10: 0984732470

Printed in the United States of America

Cover artwork by Cliff Coles & Allyson Jean Bennett

Dedication

I dedicate this book to my granddaughter Holly Mae Bennett and to the memory of my mother Phyllis Murray. Also in thankfulness for the loving arms of the Bereavement Support Group Provided by Hospice of Sacred Heart.

Acknowledgments

Thanks to photographic designer Cliff Coles and copy editor Charleynne Gates. Appreciation for the patience and critique of friends and colleagues: Jessica Maxwell, Cliff Scovell, Bob Monson, Robin Clevenger, Tom Andersen, Jon West, Kay Porter, Val Brooks, Larie Nicholas, Kirsten Steen, Tom Titus and Yvonne Young.

The Embarcadero, San Francisco

From the 1988 journal of Allyson Jean Bennett (AJB) age 24:

The #14 Mission bus is ominous as it heads toward the Ferry Building after 9:00 at night: The smell of crack [cocaine] pervades around 16th and Mission; the night-clubbers hop off at 12th for Hamburger Mary's; at 11th more disembark for the Paradise Lounge and the Oasis; at 9th some leave for Lips Underground; the coach is left with the more down-and-out elements of life who exit at various blocks for the residential hotels, for the Greyhound station at 7th street, for more residential hotels, for a few final bars, and then most everyone else is off at the Transbay Bus Terminal for points east, north, south, maybe west, I don't know, but that's where the last of this night's riders depart the #14 Mission.

Except I stay to the end of the line, a few blocks down. This is where the briefcases stream earlier in the day--clicking of heels-- ties, skirts and tennis shoes bustle about, but a ghost town after 9:00 at night, it feels.

When I exit, it is as if I enter a wasteland but I quickly cross the street to the walkway...on the Embarcadero heading toward the Bay Bridge, the water is a glimmering jewel laid out before me. The traffic streams above on the freeway, creating a steady hum. Below, there are few if any pedestrians in sight. The lights on the bridge [reflect] in the water. As I approach, I can hear the waves lapping against the cement wall and the salt smell and damp air calms me. As I walk along next to the rail a sense of peace envelops, the steady traffic provides no threat, and the few people in sight are sharing the view or are curled up in sleeping bags against the wall snoring loudly.

I think it must be a false sense of security. *It only takes one crazy to hurt you, and in such a deserted area there's no hope for rescue.* But I can't help feeling that if I were homeless this is where I would sleep. As I walk toward the bridge the water in front of me continues to sparkle, but when I turn to look back, the light no longer reflects and it is as though a darkness grows behind me as I pass into light before me. I hope this isn't metaphorical or something. I'd hate to have darkness follow me everywhere I went.

Part One

Chapter One

The Death

In my garage/workshop, the unpainted puppet heads stood, each on a stick, in a clump like so many candy apples at a fair. It was Sunday afternoon, April 21st , 1991, at 4:00 p.m. I was mixing gesso, listening to NPR and selecting just the right old paintbrush to basecoat the *papier mache'* heads.

The project was to make a set of Dracula puppets for my granddaughter, Holly Bennett, my son's eleven-year-old daughter. On my last visit to her home in Texarkana, Texas, we had co-written a puppet script for Dracula. We needed the following characters: Lucy, Jonathan, her lover, and Dr.Van Helsing, her father. We also required the butler, the cook, and the gardener, who does some gruesome digging, and a maid who foolishly lets the dreaded changeable bat into Lucy's room. And of course we had to have one humanlike Count Dracula and one in the persona of a bat. Holly has always been a fan of all things gory and scary.

I blame the white-snake of the telephone for killing my daughter. This innocent piece of plastic, a chunky white desk phone, had been moved onto the workbench in the garage.

The answer is—"In the garage with the telephone!"

The phone, burst forth, ringing loudly, its white cord snaking past the electric grinding wheel, between the pots of paintbrushes, and behind the several oil cans, to the phone-jack on the wall. I believe if I hadn't answered the phone that Allyson would still be alive, but I did answer. It struck her dead, leaving me in ribbons.

The audience yelled, "Don't answer the phone!"

"Is this Celeste Rose?"

"Yes." I was always suspicious of solicitors.

"This is police officer Raymond Stearns in San Francisco."

My mind flashed, She's dead.

"Is your daughter Allyson Bennett?"

"Yes."

"Is anyone with you?"

Renters were in my house but I was alone in the garage. "Yes." I said.

"Please sit down."

I pulled the step-stool close and perched. I spoke into the phone, "She's dead, isn't she?" I offered. "She died during an epilepsy seizure?"

Raymond Stearns said, "Yes, that's possible. We're doing an autopsy. Now listen to me. Do you have paper and something to write with?"

I had a legal pad on the workbench. I moved the rack of puppet heads toward the back and pulled forward a collection of yellow pencils, whittled to uneven points.

"Yes."

"We have taken her body to the morgue. As I said, we intend to perform an autopsy. She will be at the downtown police station on McAllister between Van Ness and Polk Streets. Today is Sunday so we are not open, but you can come tomorrow and sign the paperwork to pick up her body."

"Yes," I said.

"Mrs. Rose, did you write that down."

"Yes."

"Did you understand the location?"

"Yes. At the San Francisco downtown police station, in the morgue."

"That's right. It's through the courthouse and across a breezeway. Now go and find someone to help you. You understand? You need help now. I'm sorry to have to be the one to tell you this news. Very sorry for your loss, Ma'am."

He made me write down a phone number and then he hung up. I rested the receiver back into its cradle. The white desk phone received the news unchanged. It sat on the cluttered workbench, a white desk phone with black paint spots on it, sawdust nestled between the keypads. The white cord lay unmoving in its serpentine path, quietly digesting the news before slithering away to take a nap.

Always careful with my brushes, I cleaned the gesso brush and balanced it on an empty can to dry. My scene painting teacher, Jerry Williams, would be proud. I walked away from Dracula and all his cast to step up the two stairs to the laundry room and enter the shared kitchen of my rooming house. Suzette, my renter, stood in the dining room ready to do battle with whatever drama was assailing her that day. She looked at me, her flat chest heaving with emotion, her scarred upper lip drawn tight as a result of several cleft pallet surgeries in her childhood. I communicated in staccato phrases. "Allyson's dead. In San Francisco. Died during seizure."

Suzette knew all about seizures. Her mother had epilepsy. As the oldest of nine children, Suzette had helped her father run the household while her mother had been continually ill from one thing and another, mostly reactions to anti-seizure medicines or recovering from the "fits" themselves. Suzette, for once, was speechless. Who could speak? What could be said? We just stood there with the news clouding the air between us.

I said, "Blanket." Soon I was wrapped and set in a wooden armchair with the telephone in front of me. My mind tried to plan the next twenty-four hours. *I can attach my utility trailer to my car and drive from Eugene over the Siskiyou Pass into California. I can empty Allyson's apartment and bring her things home. But the car needed repair. I had been waiting for the clutch to break so I could have it fixed. I could not pull a trailer with that car to California now. I can fly tonight to San Francisco and tomorrow I can rent a truck to drive her things home. I can drive her home. Get her home. If I get her home then I can fix her.*

Fogged-in with this noxious cloud, I called my brothers but didn't call my eighty-two year old mother. Called Rosa Kocher, my former renter and friend, in San Francisco. Called Barbara Snow, my sister-like friend, in Eugene. Later, wearing a blanket with Barbara beside me, I walked on the jogging path beside the stream to the convenience store, bought a half-gallon of milk. I needed to move. *Keep moving, they won't hit me again.* My face was puffy, my eyes red, my hair wild. I held the blanket closed with a tight fist as we stepped forward in our moccasins along this trail of tears to home. My mind and my voice repeated with my steps. "I have lived too long. I have lived too long. I have lived too long." I think, *I'm still alive with my daughter dead, that seems against nature, the child should outlive the parent.*

Dr. Winston Maxwell, my brother, cancelled his patients for the next three days and went with me on a Monday morning commuter flight from Eugene to San Francisco. My preacher brother, Farley Maxwell, said that he would go if needed.

One big mistake was that I should not have been left alone that Sunday night. Someone should have been there beside me or nearby. My bed was no comfort, the non-sleep no refuge. I was doomed to consciousness. At four a.m. I made calls to North Carolina, spreading the news to old friends in Raleigh, where we used to live.

Winston and I took extra empty luggage--large bags with smaller bags inside. We planned to bring some of Allyson's things home. The year was 1991, no charge for checked luggage.

Do people who have lost their minds select clothes to wear? Is it possible for those people to pack a toothbrush, make-up, underpants? What need had I for normal anything? I will wear any shoes, any pants, a baggy sweater, a brimmed felt hat. But I did pack. I folded the raspberry-colored coat/cloak that Allyson gifted to me and a purple dress.

I cannot go empty handed. I have to hold on—hold on to something. So I took a small dancing doll, a little skinny-legged ballerina rag doll with satin slippers. I grasped her tightly and swung her legs while I sat in my brother's car, while I waited at the airport, while I sat in the plane looking out at the near dark of this early morning in April. When the plane was in the air I pulled the tray-table down and set the doll to dancing in front of my eyes. The last time I saw Allyson, we were dancing.

     *   *   *

May, 1990 I came to San Francisco. I paid $1,000 for the two of us to attend a dance workshop with Gabrielle Roth. Allyson and I crossed the Golden Gate Bridge to a meeting room in Mill Valley. A warm-up team was there to get us ready to move.

We moved to music, stretching and walking to the rhythms. We met the other dancers. Allyson wore a bright yellow cutaway tee shirt and black tights. Her long henna hair was pulled back in a ponytail. She is short, I think, 5' 4" or something. She never packed on extra weight like I do, but then she is not a skinny rail either. She had beautiful big breasts but small enough not to sag. She had freckles on her nose, pixie ears, chubby cheeks and a nice little cleft in her chin. She was cute. And oh, she didn't like being cute. She wanted to be mysterious and exotic, thus the long henna hair. Her best feature, according to her, were her green eyes. She highlighted them with green eye shadow and dark eyeliner. With her "San Francisco vogue" dress style and at the age of twenty-six, she had made it to "sophisticated," she wished, but people still called her "cute" which "really bugged" her.

Myself? I have thin, mousy-colored hair. I'm taller than Allyson. I say 5' 8", but that's just because of the weight charts. I've been overweight throughout my life, but through constant worry and dieting I managed to keep the grossly obese woman confined to her closet. I've always been a dancer. As a teen-ager in Eugene I studied modern dance, Martha Graham style, and then as a married lady in North Carolina I took ballet lessons and wore pink tights over my fat thighs and a black leotard stretched over my double D sized breasts. I never could get my truck-like body off the ground for a decent leap.

In the Gabrielle Roth workshop I think, *I'm old for this*, I was just over fifty years old, and the others were thirty-somethings and younger. We danced. We practiced shamanistic movement. Speaking only for myself and not for Allyson, what I understood of the weekend was to move until you push through your thoughts and restrictions. Your body goes through gyrations and steps in repeated patterns until your mind clears for automatic movements, called "authentic movements," to come through. We were encouraged to vocalize.

Allyson really needed this. She had been through four years of college and four years of job-hunting and working in San Francisco. She was, at that time, working for a financial organization as a file clerk. "I get so bored, but Mr. Jeffries is really nice, though. He's like a grandpa. He likes me partly because he knows I have epilepsy and one of his own daughters has seizures."

*   *   *

Allyson had so many dreams and ambitions. She was busy following one idea after another. She was a painter, a writer, a filmmaker. At Mills College she had difficulties pinning down a major. She called me, "I can't stand this. It's not what I want. Next year I'm changing to psychology."

Later, "I've found what I want to do. I want to be an urban anthropologist."

By the fourth year she was in agony. I said, "Allyson, you don't have to graduate. Just take time off. Don't torture yourself."

"No, no, I'll finish. Otherwise, I'll lose my scholarship."

In June of 1986 she graduated with a B.A. in Sociology.

After graduation she worked at Clyde's Specialty Coffee Shop, and then as a file clerk. "Mom, who can live in San Francisco with this kind of income? It's so expensive." In order to afford to live in the city, she had to rent single rooms with shared kitchens and baths. She lived with musician drug dealers in the Haight district; in a rooming house with an elderly Chinese man who couldn't piss straight and kept hitting the wall all around the toilet. Lastly she tried running her own house-share, where people moved in and out, skipped the rent, and eventually one crazed woman began a voodoo campaign against Allyson and against me. Allyson telephoned. "Mom, be careful. There's this crazy woman who got ahold of your photo and is sticking pins in it and chanting curses."

*   *   *

At the shamanic dance workshop we changed partners and danced, "Now try moving using only your elbows," the instructors said. "Touch each other with your elbows and draw designs in the air with your elbows." Then we danced with our knees, with our butts, with our heads. The music blasted forth. Skinny Gabrielle Roth danced with abandon, wearing workout suits of swirled silver and blue metallic with cream-colored insets.

At one point she shared with us. "My father has recently died. I came from my home in New Jersey to California to be with him. Sometimes he could see me. He knew who I was. Other times he was not conscious but I sat beside him and held his hand. I continued to talk to my father. ' I am here; it's me, Gabrielle. I danced for you today, Dad. I danced you across the river, I danced you into the sky.'"

Allyson had a good time. It was a relief for her to move and get physically tired. It was a relief from working as a file clerk and serving up latte's. She let her hair down and worked out all the office-creepy-crawlies that drove her nuts. As for me, I could only think about the huge amount of money I had spent on this dance class and how the music was too loud and Gabrielle was too skinny.

*   *   *

I remembered on another occasion where Allyson and I danced together in a video booth at the Exploratorium in San Francisco. As we danced a screen showed our movements, present and past, and the echoed gestures were shown in different neon colors. We had so much fun that people became really mad at us for taking so much time on the exhibit. But we laughed and just kept dancing.

*   *   *

I moved the pink-haired rag doll on the tray-table and looked out at the sun shining on the wing of the airplane. I want to push the plane onward to take me to my daughter. Then I unfolded this essay that Allyson wrote. She had mailed me a copy a couple of years ago, which I had folded into her birth certificate and her out-of-date passport. This morning I put some of her papers in my oversized purse.

Why I Like Patsy Cline

Allyson Jean Bennett – AJB: August 26, 1989

I was pretty miserable as a child. When I was a toddler my mother dressed me in cute little bonnets, [the brims] worked wonderfully to shield me from the world. On Sundays I was left in the church nursery school only to stand in the middle of the room with my head down, hiding behind my bonnet, until my parents came back to get me. The teachers would try to play with me but would finally focus their energy on less neurotic children.

I even refused to smile at the clown at the Pullen Park carousel as he crawled on the ground looking up under my bonnet. I just turned my back [with my] head down.

I hated preschool, [three times a week], but my mother chased me around the family station wagon to get me there. The teacher [Miss Alan] seemed really big and didn't understand me, and the kids were so mean. I remember it all like a surreal dream.

Wherever I went as a child, I felt no one liked me. I never fit in. I was stupid and bad at sports. And I always felt different than the other kids.

But my mother persevered. She didn't want a child handicapped by shyness. So she made me go places, do things, and talk to people. What I remember is a multitude of painful experiences that she forced me into, such as making me go to the counter at Burger King and tell them [that] they'd given me the wrong burger. I could have died. One thing I say for this time is I learned how to be alone. I learned to entertain myself with my daydreams. [Even today] I can sit and stare for hours appearing to do nothing. At school, I always got in trouble. "Allyson is a good student, daydreams too much." My fantasies were wonderful stories that lasted for days in which I had adventures with the characters from the books I read.

I finally came out of my shell when I started dancing in the fifth grade, and doing theatre soon after. The dark shadow that covers my early childhood memories began to lift then and I began to enjoy life. I also learned to act, so that I learned to act confident and assertive, even though I was inherently shy.

When trying to feel for my greatest problem, all I could think is what makes me cry? Everything else is cerebral, a temporary problem to be solved with a little determination. But what makes me cry is the aloneness I've felt since I hid behind my bonnet. I've had only a few good friends, I never hung out in groups much but always have known many people. An orbit not willing to stick to one clique, always with a couple of friends and acquaintances with their group. I never could fit into one type of group, groups are boring, people are interesting. I love to go to movies alone, cafés, and walks alone. I learned early on to enjoy alones, but sometimes I don't want that. As independent as I am, I've always been happiest when I've had one best friend or lover. This seems idiotic to say this is my greatest problem. I can live with it. I'm not anorexic, codependent, or substance abusive, I have a healthy addiction to coffee and chocolate. When men treat me like crap, I dump them. So as clichéd as it is I have to say aloneness is my "deepest" problem, so much so that I cry when I hear Patsy Cline and especially when I'm feeling melancholy I make a special trip to Café Soma to stare into space and play every Patsy Cline song on the jukebox, twice, till I'm sufficiently intoxicated with my own misery.

*   *   *

Yes, she was shy. As a little girl in Raleigh, North Carolina, she cowered behind my leg and peeked out at people. I thought that it would *help* if I signed her up for dance classes, an activity popular in the South. The first year she learned the Russian dance from the *Nutcracker;* another time she danced the part of the prince. Dancing and the children's theatre helped her to stand up straight, to enter rooms and to meet people without cringing. But she remained shy. I think that inside she was always lonely and fearful.

Chapter Two

The Morgue

Our carry-ons over our shoulders, we snagged the four empty bags from the baggage claim and walked out, climbed into a shuttle bus and were driven to the city hall building, Van Ness and Polk. With the numerous bags in hand, we entered the front door of the city hall and ran right into a bag-inspection station. The officer in charge snapped open our large suitcases to find smaller bags inside. He hadn't seen this kind of thing before. People don't come into the courthouse with empty luggage. He poked about. I got a sick enjoyment out of telling him. "My daughter has died, her body is in your morgue, we brought these bags with us so that later we can clean out her apartment."

My brother and I looked like refugees. I had on a wide-brimmed felt hat and gray clothes, we wore warm Oregon winter coats, and were burdened by suitcases.

The officer was sympathetic. "Sorry for your loss. Good luck."

We followed the signs to the morgue and ran into a second bag-inspection station. This lady officer there was not so polite; she seemed irritated at our weird situation. We were inspected twice on the way to the morgue.

We entered through a heavy glass door into a hallway, then into the morgue office to our left. Inside was a large glass wall facing the early morning sun. I felt like a guppy inside a fish bowl. Behind the long counter stood rows of shelves against a wall. It looked like a kind of post office. The shelves held the personal effects of the dead people that were in the morgue. I identified myself and spoke the name of my daughter. "Allyson Bennett. I'm her mother, I would like to see her."

"Wait here, I'll get her things."

"I want to see her."

"Yes, I understand. I'll see if something can be arranged."

It is Monday morning in San Francisco, another busy weekend for the police station and for the morgue.

The lady gave me a large envelope and I signed to acknowledge the receipt. There was a wallet, an address book, a ring and a watch. I put the ring on my pinkie finger, the watch on my left wrist and the wallet and address book into my own purse. Other people were in the room, all waiting to claim their bodies.

I became agitated. I knew that I was very close to Allyson and I couldn't stand not to be with her. I asked again, "I would like to see my daughter."

"Oh, I'm afraid that's not possible, and besides, you don't want to see her. She is not in very good shape. It's better if you wait until the funeral home fixes her up a little bit."

"I don't care what she looks like, I have to see her now." I raised my voice and was beginning to be hysterical. "I want my daughter, right here, right now. I don't care what condition she is in, I want to touch her."

"Believe me, lady, you don't want to see her. Have the funeral home pick her up later today. Besides, they've just started the autopsy."

"I've been here a half an hour. I wasn't too late to see her then."

"Have a seat. There's nothing you can do now."

"If I can't see her let me touch the outside of the wall where she is. I want her to know that I am here." Progressively I began to be really upset, my actions growing into full out ranting and raving. I gave everyone in the room a good look at raw emotions. "This is unnatural, to keep a mother away from her dead child's body. Is this what you call an advanced civilization? To keep us separated? I belong by her side. This is not right. It is inhumane. It is grotesque."

All this time my brother Winston remained quiet. He gave me the dignity of letting me express my needs and wants. At last he came to retrieve me from the counter. "Come, Sis, sit down here a minute." He helped me cross to the row of metal and plastic chairs where I sat, trembling and shaking. He talked softly into my ear. "There's nothing you can do. Maybe we should go now."

As adults my brothers never called me Sis or Sister. In everyday life we used our names to one another. The term Sis or Sister was an endearment that was saved for high holy days.

My brother and I and our six bags went back through the inspection-points towards the city street. Incredibly the officials searched us again and all six of our bags. They were not impressed by my tale of woe.

We rode a taxi to 949 Capp Street #38, one block from Mission Street. This was Allyson's new apartment. I hadn't seen it yet. She had a career-path job at last as an administrative assistant for the American Foundation for the Blind. She could now afford a studio apartment with a separate kitchen, walk-in closet, bathroom, and a San Francisco bay window with long lace curtains. The young lady apartment manager trembled with nervousness. "I'm so sorry for you. You're the mother? God, this is just awful."

"Yes, it is horrible." Winston said, "It's helpful that you are here to let us in."

"God, I can't believe she's dead, she was such a nice person. Really friendly and everything." It was the young manager's first death in her building. Allyson's door was difficult to open. We each tried the key. A person had to pull up on the doorknob at the same time as turning the lock. There was yellow tape across the door. The police had been there the day before.

*   *   *

Sonja and Janet were worried when Allyson did not show up for her exam. They were all members of the NSA Buddhists, Nichiren Shoshu of America. NSA exams were something that they have to struggle with. They had been preparing for the exams.

Saturday night, Allyson had gone home early because she didn't feel well. She had a pre-seizure feeling and wanted to be by herself.

Sonja and Janet called from time to time during the night and on Sunday morning, before and after the Buddhist exam. Allyson did not pick up. They had talked to her answer-machine:

Jazz music played, followed by Allyson's voice: "Hi, you've reached 641-4557. Thank you for calling, please leave a message. Bye." Jazz music…

#1. "Allyson, this is Sonja, it's nine o'clock. I'll be going to bed shortly, so call me in the morning, I should be up about 8 o'clock. Good-bye."

#2. "Allyson, it's Janet. We're here chanting away, wondering where you are at. Maybe you're chanting at your house. Please call back and let me know what's happening. If you need a ride and all that sort of stuff." (Sounds worried, crying?) "Thank you very much."

#5. Click and hang up.

#6. Click and hang up.

Sonja is a pistol-packing welfare cop and had made many emergency house- calls to the poor and desperate. She and Janet were concerned. They decided to go to Allyson's apartment to check things out. The same young manager struggled with the lock. It was Sunday morning just before eleven o'clock. The door popped open and a blast of heat with a horrible smell came rolling out. The manager and Janet walked across the apartment to the windows and struggled to open the side casements of the old bay windows. In the kitchen, Janet found the remains of a teakettle melted onto the stove with gas flames going full power beneath it. On the round table by the kitchen window was an empty cup with a coffee funnel, containing the makings of a rich cup of coffee. Because of her epilepsy, Allyson only allowed herself two vices, cigarettes and good dark coffee. She had recently stopped the cigarettes and added a healthy bi-weekly swim at the local gym.

Sonja found the body. "Here she is," she yelled out. She saw Allyson's jeans-and-Tee-shirt-clad body lying in the dry bathtub, her head cranked sideways. She had evidently had a seizure while standing at the bathroom sink and had fallen into the bathtub, hitting her head on the faucet end and twisting her neck, cutting off her breath.

*   *   *

My brother and I, accompanied by the manager struggled with the stubborn lock. The door swung wide and we could see lace curtains fluttering at the open windows. The smell was gone now but the young apartment manager seemed to still smell it. She gagged, sickened and nervous. "I'm so sorry, what happened to your daughter. When we came in here yesterday it was so hot. The stove had been on all night. There was a smell. Oh god, I'm sorry. If you need anything, I'll be in my apartment. Oh god, I'm sorry." The young woman turned and ran down the stairway behind us.

Allyson's boots lay slumped as she had left them, kicked off by the door. "Well," I said, "Here she is, here's Allyson. Her soul is right here, flapping around her brand new expensive leather boots." She had just splurged, paying $90 for a new pair of boots.

This was my first time in Allyson's new apartment. She had looked forward to my coming to see it, a studio apartment with bathroom, kitchen, and large room-sized-closet. Her things were here. Her mess was here--clothes on the floor, dirty dishes in the sink, papers strewn, writings in piles, movie cameras and lights, and by the bay window, an artist's easel with a gray and lavender acrylic painting representing standing columns. Lying on the artist's palette was a paintbrush loaded with orange paint.

I touched the handle of the brush. Saturday night she had held this brush. *Hold on to her touch, touch where she had touched.*

The telephone rang. I answered it. "It's Larry, I'm downstairs. Buzz me up."

What? Larry on the phone and here? It took me a minute to figure out the apartment system--a doorbell that rings your phone and a buzzer by the door to let your friends in through the security gate.

Larry Burnett came in. He was Allyson's ex-boyfriend. "I have my truck, I took the next few days off. I'm yours. Anything you need."

I thought. *We are not alone. Not alone in Allyson's apartment to take care of her things, we are not alone, there is support everywhere. There is help. How did I ever believe that I would have to handle this by myself?*

Winston opened up the yellow pages to mortuaries. We picked one name, *Daphne.* Maybe the name was non-Christian enough for this Buddhist girl. A piece of advice had come to me from somewhere. *Beware of Catholic mortuaries in San Francisco; some are run by the Mafia.* We drove in Larry's pick-up to Daphne's Funeral Home. The people there were Filippinos--small brown people in felt slippers quietly moving from the dead to the living, receiving the bodies, talking to the survivors in the office, pushing gurneys along the narrow hallways, preparing the dead for their ultimate journey.

Winston, Larry, and I, sat on chairs facing the director's desk. The mortician had her forms to fill out.

I broached our business, "First of all, we would like your company to pick up my daughter's body from the city morgue on Polk and Van Ness Streets."

"Yes, we would do that. Let me first say that we are so sorry for your loss. You are her mother? Could you please tell me your name?"

"I am Celeste Rose from Eugene, Oregon, and this is my Brother Winston Maxwell and our friend Larry Burnett."

"Excuse me, but we have to fill out some necessary papers. First of all, what was your daughter's name?" She asked. I noticed, with internal alarms going off, that she had used the past tense. *Your daughter's name...was...?*

I spoke. The men with me, like twin centurions, sat silently by my left side and my right side. "Her name was Allyson Jean Bennett." I gasped and quaked. Her father and I had named her, now I un-name her in death. "A-l-l-y-s-o-n. I wanted the 'y' in her name to give her signature some drama."

*   *   *

I remembered that wee baby. She was four pounds eight ounces, a little bit too small, so that the hospital had to put her into an isolette. There had been some damage to the placenta. Perhaps she had been mal-nourished. Is that where the killer epilepsy had come from? A birth defect planted inside her electrical systems that would cause trouble when she turned eighteen? Isn't that a fairy tale? The witch's curse? *When she is sixteen she will prick her finger on a spindle and die.* Lawton Bennett, my former husband, and I had wanted this, our second child, so much. Our son, Max, was born when I was just twenty. He was healthy and easy. Allyson seemed to take so long to even get started. It was more than three years of trying before I even got pregnant again, four years between our children.

I stayed at home and rocked the baby all that winter. I used to sit in the Kennedy rocking chair overlooking the little Beaver Dam Creek valley. I watched the squirrels running along their winding roads on the bare limbs of the tulip poplar trees.

*   *   *

I answered more questions, "Born January 3, 1964. Raleigh, North Carolina." Now I give a death date. "Died in San Francisco, California, April 21, 1991." *Oh dear. That is my ex-husband's birthday.* Poor Lawton Bennett, what a thing for him to always remember.

"What was her occupation?"

I smiled and looked at Larry. "Not a secretary." I said. "Administrative Assistant? Oh no, she wasn't just a secretary. She was a college graduate, an artist, a dancer, a writer, a filmmaker." I asked Larry, "What was her occupation?"

He couldn't speak. He slumped down in his chair, "Movies?" He whispered.

"Author of screen plays." I said.

"Do you have special requests for the burial preparations?"

"What's that called? Cremation. No casket, no embalming, just lay her out on a table." I thought and then continued, "No clothes, just a winding sheet. Larry what do you think?"

He said, his voice husky, "Her Buddhist beads."

"Yes, her Buddhist beads held in her hands, we'll bring them, her hair hanging down, long, over the end of the table. She has beautiful henna-colored hair. "

The kind and gentle funeral director said, "We will pick up her body at the city morgue."

"Could I see her as soon as possible?"

"Yes, you can have a viewing, I think, at 4:00 this afternoon."

I thought. We can make this into a song:

> *Pick her up at the City Morgue*
> *Drive her down the city streets.*
> *Everyone gather in the afternoon,*
> *See our girl in her winding sheet.*

There is no need for a casket, she wanted to be cremated, I think. I snap to all these decisions. I feel like I was plugged into Allyson's knowledge bank. I knew what she wanted and needed. I answered with confidence. We had formed a committee-- God, Allyson and me, or was it Buddha? I don't even know who Buddha is. I began making these decisions by checking in with the committee, gaining confidence as I went. I spoke and acted one way. Then as the grieving mother, I acted another way, often collapsing and crying.

"We have no crematorium in San Francisco," said the funeral director. "She will have to go to Marin County. There is a waiting list. Perhaps it will be a week or more."

She will have to go? I visualized a line of hearses, the Golden Gate Bridge in the background, waiting in line for the crematorium. *Oh, the big city, you even have to wait in line to be cremated,* however, dead people are most likely a very patient group.

The discussion of the viewing of the body was too much for poor Larry. It was his turn to collapse and sob.

I spoke on the phone to Mary, my sister-in-law. She's an RN and my weight loss sister. I pleaded, "Mary, I don't know what to eat."

"Try to eat your normal food at the usual time. Don't eat anything strange. Try to keep a schedule." I'm the kind of overweight person that does not make good food choices. Especially when I am under stress. Larry, Winston, and I went out to lunch after the mortuary. I had steamed vegetables and pasta with no sauce, just something basic. It was so strange to take time out to eat. *Why are we eating and Allyson is dead? Living people eat. Dead people don't.*

We went back to the apartment. Larry said, "Call me if you want anything." And he turned his back on this scene. He seemed to be having a difficult time dealing with these darker facts of life. People die and sometimes they are people that we love, sometimes they are people we used to love.

Winston and I rested and made phone calls. I opened my daughter's calendar planner and made some calls to cancel her appointments. I don't remember talking to the people at her office.

With Sonja on the phone, we were told that her friends had planned a memorial service at the home of a Buddhist chief for Tuesday night. They informed me that a private ritual would take place here, this evening, at Allyson's *gohonzon*, her altar.

The Buddhist religion has definite procedures for being born and dying. In her checkbook I noticed that Allyson had just made the last payment on her *gohonzon*, a beautiful wooden shelf with a cabinet on the top. There were doors to open that revealed a red silk scroll within. At home Allyson was a slob; however, around her altar everything was clean and neat. There was a vase of fresh green leaves, a bowl of fruit, a tray of incense ashes, a bell, a gong. Several times a day, she would kneel on a prayer rug there and bow, then holding her hands together in prayer, she rattled her beads, (clacking the beads together, slipping both hands smoothly up and down.) She would sound the gong and open the doors of her personal altar.

The whole of last year she had continually prayed for personal healing from epilepsy and for peace on earth. She had chanted fervently for the end of fighting during the Gulf War, repeating her mantra for peace. Years before she had rejoiced when the Berlin Wall had come down. She had demonstrated against nuclear bombs and had been arrested in the deserts of Nevada. She had been so proud of being arrested. I was proud that she wore my huge oversized wool coat during the protest. I remembered that as a baby in North Carolina, we carried her when our family had marched for racial justice and equality, singing "We Shall Overcome."

One of the Buddhist chants is "*nam myoho renge kyo.*" Allyson told me that it is part of the *Devotion to the Lotus Sutra.* This means something like, as the white lotus flower comes out of the mud, so beauty will come out of the struggles of life. This chant is repeated, over and over, hundreds of times a day, into a solid intention.

The repeated prayer to me feels like the laying of bricks and mortar. Row by row a foundation is created, building a strong hold for your faith, a place to lean on, a place to lift up your dreams, for yourself or for your planet. Then the gong is rung and other chants are offered. Allyson's *gohonzon,* her altar, contained a special red silk scroll from Japan, which represented her inner self, her particular soul, Allyson Jean Bennett in San Francisco. This night in April, her Buddhist's young women's group would enact the ritual of removing the scroll and closing the *gohonzon.*

I talked on the phone to my friend Rosa, who lives near the Presidio. She promised to join us at the mortuary to view the body at 4:00 o'clock. By this time Lawton Bennett, his new wife, Sarah, and my son Max, had arrived from Texas. They were to meet us at Daphne Funeral Home with Uncle Lynn and Aunt Jan from San Jose.

Winston and I played a Beatles tape on the sound system. Winston was wearing a leather jacket, I remember because of the smell. I was still in my gray disaster clothes but without the hat. The Beatles sang "Hey Jude, don't make it bad, take a sad song and make it better. Remember to let her into your heart and you can start to make it better." Winston hugged me, then we started swaying and we did a kind of slow dance in the apartment. "Da-da-da-da, hey Jude." Both of us cried.

This felt exceedingly sweet to me.

*   *   *

As a young woman Allyson knew a lot about rock and roll and made herself an expert on national and international groups, as well as on the local Eugene scene. During her junior year of high school she had been on the selection committee of the bands for the senior prom.

The day of the prom she was decorating the hall when a young man asked her. "Hey, Allyson, are you going to the dance?"

"No, I guess not," she answered.

"Oh , you've got to go, after all the work you've put into it. How about you go with me?"

She arrived home to our small house in West Eugene with only three hours before the prom. She carried a borrowed a dress.

She stood on the coffee table, talking and talking, telling me all about the band and the decorations and what *he* had said and what *she* had said, while I turned up the hem of the dress. A friend came and styled her hair, her date arrived, and off they went.

                    *   *   *

As a teen-ager she was interested in religion and Christianity. She went often to church and church meetings and camp. One of her best friends was her youth leader, Polly Moak.

One Christmas morning she woke up at her Uncle Farley's house on Officer's Row in Vancouver, Washington. The house was across the street from Fort Vancouver's parade grounds. There was a bum in the park curled up in a sleeping bag, white frost on the grass around him. Allyson saw him and was struck with an idea. She hurried around the house and prepared a cup of coffee for the man, put a sweet roll on a napkin and filled a Christmas stocking for him. She scooted across the street and laid the offerings by his sleeping head, so that when he awoke he had a Christmas surprise.

She chose Mills College in Oakland because they gave her a full scholarship and because they had convinced her that the atmosphere of an all-women's campus was preferable to the coed schools. She explained it to me, counting off on her slender young fingers. "At an all-women's college the smartest person in every class is a woman. The committee chairperson is a woman. The leader of every project is a woman, etc. By the time the female students graduate they are able to take the lead on any business or any other kind of opportunity." This reasoning made sense to me. She was frustrated with her major of the social sciences but she kept her interest in films, stage, and music through her extracurricular choices.

After graduation from college, she moved to the city and through her boyfriend Larry became interested in Buddhism. The young people's groups were very active in meetings and studies. The prayers and chants were intense. She chanted in the mornings and evenings and learned the liturgy from teachers. Larry was a punk -drummer-Buddhist. Later he became a UPS delivery worker. By day he kept his long hair curled under his cap and by night he let his hair down and drummed in one band or another.

One thing I really liked about Larry was the way he approached Allyson's seizures. She told me that one day in his apartment, he was chanting in front of his *gohonzon* when across the room Allyson reared back violently and had a grand mal seizure. When she came conscious again Larry was holding her and petting her sweaty head. "Were you talking to God?" he asked. I guess Julius Caesar was said to talk to the gods during moments of unconsciousness.

Chapter Three

The Viewing

On our second trip to Daphne Funeral Home, we journeyed by cab to the top of the peaceful hill where city sounds were muffled by splashing fountains, by the trees and April flowers. The small viewing rooms were on the left at the end of a long hallway. There was a comfortable parlor near by.

I looked at Winston, "I would like to be undisturbed and alone with Allyson's body as long as I want. I don't care how much time I take. Don't come in the door and don't let anyone else in the door."

Winston answered, "You got it."

The mortuary worker, this time an African-American lady with a round face and gentle eyes, said nervously, "She is discolored, uh, from the suffocation." She looked down at her hands. I had not ordered any cosmetics to be used on the body. I had not ordered embalming.

I said, "Purple, bruised?"

"There is markings and discoloration."

I went in the room. Allyson lay wrapped in a white sheet with her long henna-colored hair hanging down, neatly brushed and flowing. Her hands and bare arms were folded over her chest. Part of her face was a deep rosy color, her lips were black and there were dark maroon freckles. Half of her neck was vivid pink with more maroon freckles, the other half of her neck was creamy white. That is the way the blood pools inside a body after death. Her arms and chest were mainly white. Her eyelids were puffy, purple and again with freckles. Her black lips were large and swollen. She would be glad to know that she didn't look cute, at all. She was exotic. After the first shock, she looked beautiful to me, her mother. She had become a rare and exquisite orchid.

Her face resembled an African face—Ethiopian, Egyptian, otherworldly. When I laid my hands on her, which I did right away, she was cold and solid-feeling, as if she had transformed into marble. Through the fabric of the white sheet, I touched her body, her feet, and her thighs. I lightly stroked her hair. She lay so still--Allyson, who was such a lively person, animated, loquacious, laughing and smiling. Changed now, she was still. Allyson was not here anymore, she was gone, this was her heavy marble shell.

I put her Buddhist beads into her dead stiff hands. I looked under the sheet at her autopsy wound. I kissed her black lips. She was so beautiful, an art object, strange to me.

I pulled the chair up and sat to talk with her. I told jokes and she did not laugh. I prayed as best I could to God and the pantheon of gods surrounding us. I saw her bathed in a beautiful pink light from the angels above. She shimmered. Then when I looked up I saw the source. The ceiling had pink spotlights shining directly down onto the table. This made me laugh and I said out loud. "I see you bathed in a pink light from God and all the angels bending down to carry you home." I laughed again, but Allyson just lay there. She didn't laugh, although it was really our kind of joke.

I spoke of feelings and talked about the epilepsy and about Larry Burnett, her ex-boyfriend. Surely she would respond to talking about Larry.

I said, "He came over immediately when he heard. He drove us here this morning in his red pickup truck, and afterwards we had lunch. He is really sad. And now he's disappeared. I think he just couldn't take it. I left your message machine on. There are lots of messages coming in. Your dad and Max, Uncle Lynn and Aunt Jan. People inviting you to dance, to hang out, wondering what was happening. I like your new apartment, it's really nice. Capp Street seems to be a good place. Allyson, you are so quiet, you just lie there looking like a fabulous sculpture and you don't say anything." I talked on and on. I heard my ex-husband's voice and my son's East Texas twang. People were gathering in the parlor-- Uncle Lynn and Aunt Jan, Lawton's new wife, Sarah. I heard Winston talking to them in the next room with voices soft and muted by the walls and by the presence of death in the atmosphere of the mortuary.

I wanted to prepare Allyson for her funeral pyre. I had brought one of her hairbrushes with me. I stood at the top of the table and picked up a few strands of her hair. I tried to run the brush through it. I wanted the experience to be ritualistic and beautiful. The picture in my head was the grieving mother brushing her dead daughter's hair, the long red hair. When she was a child and a teenager, her hair had been honey blond and very thick and naturally wavy. Wonderful hair. As an adult she colored it with a dark reddish henna. The color suited her light skin and freckles. Here, I was afraid to pull on her hair. Already I felt like her body was decaying and I worried that her hair might fall out. I was afraid of the tangles in her hair and I dared not brush it vigorously. Anyway, it looked lovely just the way it was, brushed away from her purple face and flowing off the end of the table.

Allyson had great style. She had learned to dress using fashions from thrift stores. For her high-powered executive assistant job at the American Foundation for the Blind, she wore her long hair pulled back. She dressed in suits and simple dresses with scarves to add the drama that matched her personality. When she came home after work, down would come her hair and she'd tease it out. In those days people dressed in a style called "San Francisco vogue," so she would use light base make-up and dark purple or black colored lip-stick. "Look here," I said aloud. "Allyson, honey, you finally got your wish--white skin and black lips. You are beautiful, my sweet." I stopped the brushing and bent to kiss her forehead. I prepared myself to say good-bye to her. *Good-bye forever, to her body, but not to her. She will live within my heart forever*. I sat with her body a while longer but the real Allyson wasn't there. I exited the viewing room and stood in the doorway of the parlor. I made my entrance speech, a joke, of course, to cover up my nervousness.

"She's purple. She's turned into an orchid. Anyone can go see her that wants to, but prepare yourself, she's purple with pink polka dots."

Lawton Bennett, Allyson's father, and his wife, Sarah, went in. I heard them, felt them, gasp and cry. I hugged my thirty-one year old son, Max Bennett. We all sat in a circle; the light coming in through the large windows showed the hilltop garden. Uncle Lynn and Aunt Jan sat in front of the window, back lighted, appearing to me in silhouette. We talked about the death and the discovery of the body. Winston had pencil and paper and began writing Allyson's obituary.

Just as in the mortuary office that morning, when I said Allyson's full name out loud I had to "fall to pieces." I fell back in my chair and made croaking, snorting noises and began to thrash. Early on I had promised myself that I would follow through with feelings and movements. If I wanted to crawl on the floor and oink like a pig, then I would do that. I was conscious, however, of the need to look good in front of my ex-husband and his family. It was the first time that I ever saw his new wife, Sarah. Here I was in my gray distress rags with no make-up. *Oh, well.* But I was going to answer my needs for myself and not worry what anyone thought. This was not a time for appearances, and, *be damned*, I wouldn't try to hold myself together.

I envied the procedures that are in place for the Southern charismatic churches where attendants in white clothing surround the bereaved and tend to their physical needs. If a woman's skirt rose up to show too much thigh an attendant would see to her modesty. They would wipe her snot, her sweat and tears; they supported the grieving person's body when she fell backwards and keep a safe area for thrashing and kicking. Sometimes grief hits like an epileptic seizure, I think to myself, *I wish that I could have such attendants.*

Just then the front door of the building opened and down the long hall came Rosa. She is a big-city woman who walks confidently in her four-inch heels. That day she was wearing a bright red silk shirt and a black leather mini-skirt. *Here comes my team,* I thought. *Here comes my help and my support.* She swooped into the room with her flowers for Allyson. She met the others and gathered me to her.

Rosa had lived in Eugene with Allyson and me for a couple of years. She had been a student at the University of Oregon, studying landscape architecture.   We had worked on marionette shows together. We had traveled to Italy together for a summer art program. She had moved into our house and had become a sister to the young Allyson and a sister to me.   Rosa is an attractive person.   Men are drawn to her like a pilot to the sky. She is so purely sexy that even women love her.   She talks with her hands and has a soft and sophisticated voice with an accent that is totally affected. She was raised in Sacramento and as a twenty-year-old she disapproved of her own "Valley Girl" voice and set to work recording herself to improve her speech and to make her voice sound like someone from the movies. She copied the speech of people whom she admired.   Her voice is so mysterious that people often say, "Where are you from?"

Rosa has a great mane of sandy-colored hair. She is tall, long-legged, small- breasted and has expressive hands, the hands of a sculptor, designer, and massage therapist. Her fingernails are painted in bright fire-engine red.   She calls her ten red fingertips her "feathers."

Rosa and I went into Allyson's viewing room.   Rosa had bought orchids. "I was looking for roses but I couldn't find any.   I bought these Dendrobium orchids." They are small purple and white flowers on long stems. There were purple speckles on the petals.

I said, "Rosa, Allyson herself has turned into an orchid. Look at her. Forever now, these kinds of orchids will be her flowers, pale and purple, with maroon freckles."

Rosa stood beside me.   We looked down at the sleeping princess, the marble goddess. Rosa touched Allyson's cold firm body. I said, "She's turned into a marble sculpture."

"I see this too."

Rosa did as I had done and passed her hands over Allyson's cheeks, her hands, her arms, her abdomen, and legs. I thought that Rosa with her magical hands, perhaps by the power of her touch, could awaken this sleeping princess. But alas no. She talked to Allyson, much the same way that I had earlier, she stroked and kissed her.

I told Rosa the joke about the pink lights and Rosa laughed loudly. In the parlor the gathering mourners might have heard the laughter coming from the viewing room. "What do you want to do?" Rosa asked.

"I want you to rock me."

She pulled another chair up by Allyson's viewing table. Rosa sat down beside me and I leaned onto her lap. She rocked me, crooning, "My sweet, my darling, rest in my arms. You are safe and you are loved, Allyson is with us now and will be with us in our hearts. Sweet, my love." She began to sing, in her off-pitch, husky voice, one of her pagan songs. "The earth is our mother, she will take care of you. The earth is our mother, she will take care of you."

When at last I felt satisfied that it was enough, the time had come for final parting, We turned our backs on Allyson's shell, her remains, and we walked away forever, never to see her or touch her again. Her next stop would be a crematorium in Marin County.

Chapter Four

The Viewing Dinner Party

Everyone went out to supper after the viewing. I remember us: myself, Dr. Winston Maxwell, M.D., Dr. Lawton Bennett, Ph.D., Sarah Bennett, my son Maxwell Stuart Bennett, brother to the deceased, Lynn Bennett, Jan Bennett, and (Bunny) Rosa Kocher all riding in Lynn's sedan, three in the front and five in the back

We decided on Italian food. "I know a place, called North Beach Restaurant. Best Italian food in San Francisco," said Uncle Lynn, and off we drove, making several passes at the Italian neighborhood. After the third time around Telegraph Hill, one of the women said.

"Why don't we stop and ask directions?"

"I know where it is," answered Uncle Lynn.

"Yes, yes. Besides you're a guy and everyone knows that guys don't ask for directions." Good-hearted derision and laughter followed.

The back seat was crowded. My son, Winston, and I were the base support with Rosa and Aunt Jan on our laps. The two women were tall enough that their necks bent into the upholstered roof of the sedan. Driving up and then down the hills of San Francisco, the car turned right and left, climbing and descending, our bodies in the back seat pressed up, down, and sideways. Someone leaned an elbow into my gray brimmed felt hat, smushing it down over my eyes.

"It's around here somewhere," said Uncle Lynn. He's also the kind of guy who insists on paying the whole check.

We unloaded out of the sedan, clown style, in front of North Beach Restaurant, the pedestrians on the street got a real show. We stood in front of the windows, patting down our clothes waiting for Uncle Lynn to park and meet us.

The restaurant staff quickly organized a table for eight. It had a festive look in the middle of the crowded restaurant. I took off my sad hat, fluffed my thin, limp, hair and stood up. I rang the water glass near me, touched Allyson's ring for courage, checked her watch on my wrist for the time. We had to be back at the apartment before 8:00 o'clock because Allyson's Buddhist women's group was coming to ceremonially remove the red-silk scroll from her *gohonzon*. I spoke out. "Hear ye, hear ye! We are here to celebrate Allyson's life and to mourn her death." I was in my performance mode, no need for crying. "I want it to be known..." and I looked boldly at my former brother-in-law, Lynn Bennett, and emphasized my words. "I want it to be known that Allyson will be thrilled to at last have enough money to buy everyone's meal tonight. As you all know, she had finally landed her career-path job, and there is plenty of insurance money to pay for one and all."

Wine, purchased by Uncle Winston, was poured and toasts were made, clinking glasses all around. Rosa reached to my hand and touched Allyson's gold ring. It had an abstract of a face on it. I said, "You take it, Rosa. You should wear her ring."

"No, no, honey, you need to keep it."

"Here." I took off the ring and put it part way on one of Rosa's manicured fingers.

"Thank you, I shall wear it with pride and many happy memories." She kissed me on both cheeks, Italian style. "You know, Allyson came to my house last week. She called and said she wanted to come over. Maybe it was Saturday or Sunday night, just last week. We walked up to the Presidio and sat on the wall overlooking the ocean. I felt like she was saying good-bye. She hadn't been to see me for months and months. The sun was setting and we watched to see if there would be any pretty clouds. Like she was sailing into the sunset."

Winston said, "Spumoni, it's Italian, we have to have spumoni ice cream."

Rosa's dramatic voice spoke out, "No, no, Winston! We have to have gelato. Raspberry gelato."

Everyone argued. "Spumoni, gelato, spumoni, gelato, spumoni…"

I said, "Order what you will." And everyone did that.

Chapter Five

Night at the Apartment

Everyone, squishing into the sedan again, came with us to the apartment. We entered from Capp Street through the wrought-iron Spanish-style gate and into the entry hall, damp and cold like an ancient crypt. We walked up the two flights. Her apartment was at the front of the building at the turn of the hall.

Brother Winston struggled with the eccentric lock and key. I turned to the family and apologized, "I'm sorry. We were here earlier today and the place is a terrible mess." Everyone laughed and remembered their own stories abut Allyson's jumbled living conditions. We called it "gerbil décor."

Entering Allyson's home again, this time with the family, we passed the room-sized walk-in closet on the right and a bathroom on the left. Her $90 boots lay by the door. The living room-bedroom combination had bay windows that faced Capp Street. In the lace-curtained window space was a card table and the oil painting in progress. There was an old-fashioned traveling trunk, a chair and a bookshelf.

Filling the long wall of the room was a futon couch, a table with a sculptured head on it and an old-fashioned wooden wheel-chair parked to the side for extra seating. I hated this wheelchair décor; I thought that it had bad *Karma*. Across on the left wall were more bookshelves and then the sudden island of cleanliness and order where Allyson had placed her meticulously-kept Buddhist altar, the *gohonzon*, with the prayer rug on the floor. Off this room on the left was the kitchen with another smaller bay window. The melted teakettle stood to one side of the stovetop.

Her dad, Lawton, and his wife, Uncle Lynn and Jan, Rosa, my son Max, and my brother Winston, all found places to sit and everyone was stiff and solemn, as if in church. We waited for the Buddhist women's group to arrive.

Her friends told me that Allyson had felt sick, thought she might be going to have an epileptic seizure. She had a seizure four weeks before after a whole year of being incident-free. She needed to adjust her medicine again.

Five of her Buddhist friends came in, including Sonja and Janet, whom I had already met by telephone. The family and the guests wept and whispered to each other in the ragged circle. Leetho, the woman with the Buddhist book paged through to the reading for the ceremony.

The Buddhist women kneeled down facing the *gohonzon* and chanted, bowing their heads and rattling their prayer beads between their hands, *"Nam myoho renge kyo. Nam myoho renge kyo. Nam myoho renge kyo,"* repeating this mantra perhaps a hundred times. They bowed again and sounded the gong to signal the respectful opening, for the last time, of Allyson's altar. They prayed, taking turns, reading from the small red book.

Leetho explained to us, "This is for the occasion of removing the scroll and disassembling her altar because of her death." Her voice choked with tears.

Carol said, "I'm sorry, but we have never performed this ceremony before. Our teacher, our Buddhist chief, has given us the instructions just this afternoon." They opened the *gohonzon* and took out Allyson's scroll and rolled it tightly. Cheryl handed the five-inch scroll with the yellow tasseled end to Carol, Leetho held out a long narrow red silk pouch, and Carol slipped the scroll inside.

There were more prayers and then the ashes from the incense were scooped into a box to be given to Larry. Larry was Allyson's first teacher in the faith. Carol continued, "This small scroll will be sent back to Japan. If Allyson's relative, for instance one of you, like her mother, father, niece Holly or brother Max, wanted to become a Buddhist you could use the same scroll. It will be kept there in Japan under her name. Now that the scroll has been removed, the altar is no longer sacred. It is only wood and metal."

"What should we do with the altar?" I asked.

Sonja said, "Perhaps you could give it to Allyson's student. She was teaching a young lady at the center."

"I think that would be a good thing. Does anyone of the family want the *gohonzon*?"

"Give it to her student," said Allyson's dad, finally speaking out. He had been so quiet, somewhat disabled by his recent stroke and disheartened by this death of his daughter. *Disheartened is a mild word. Ripout-hearted would be better.* Allyson's Buddhist friends said their good-byes, invited us all to the memorial service at the chief's house tomorrow, and left the apartment.

The family stood and looked at one another. I said, taking charge as usual, "Tomorrow we need to go through her things. We have three days to empty the apartment. We could meet after 9:00 o'clock? Here?"

Aunt Jan spoke up, "I'll bring everyone in. Lynn is working tomorrow."

Max and Rosa stayed at the apartment with Winston and me. Rosa boiled water for tea, using a simple saucepan. We all looked at the ruined teakettle, an innocent victim of Saturday night's disaster.

My son was quiet. He sat on the end of the futon and looked through Allyson's music tapes. I had to talk and decided to narrate the scene as I patched together the order of events using physical evidence, the answer machine, the comments of her Buddhist friends, the kicked-off $90 boots, the burnt teakettle, the paint brush, and the paint rag. I told the story partly for the others, but mostly for myself.

"She felt pre-seizure, so she came home. She came in the door." I nodded to the apartment entrance. "She kicked off her new boots, there, just inside. She walked through the apartment to the kitchen and filled the teakettle with water from the tap and turned the gas-fed flames on high. She selected a mug from the drain board, probably a dirty mug because the cabinets were empty and the sink was full of dirty dishes. She put the coffee funnel and filter on top. She took some of her special 'Allyson's Blend' coffee and measured out two and a half teaspoons. She walked out of the kitchen to the bay window. Moving the card table an inch or two, and looking at the over-head light, she adjusted the acrylic painting on its table-top easel and picked up a wide flat brush and loaded it with orange paint straight from the tube. Paint rag in her hand, she walked the few steps to the bathroom. She went in and pulled down her jeans to pee, then, after zipping up her pants, she stood with her back to the old-fashioned footed tub and washed her hands. She ran the paint rag under the spigot and rung out the extra water.

"She began her seizure as she always did, by bending forward with a contraction in her mid-section. Then her body snapped back, torpedo-like, into an arc. Leading with her head, she propelled herself into the faucet end of the dry bathtub. She hit her head, and with one blue-jean leg sticking out over the edge, she jerked, then rocked gently against the front end of the tub with her head bent at an acute angle as she was holding her breath. When she relaxed into unconsciousness, she ceased breathing. She couldn't breathe and then she died. The teakettle began to scream. Allyson's spirit, still connected somewhat to her body, heard the whistle. 'Oh, shit!' her spirit said, 'the teakettle, I can't take it off the stove!' The teakettle screamed and screamed and then it stopped but the flame kept on, melting the metal kettle into the iron eye of the gas range and heating the room hotter and hotter. The phone rang. It was her other friend, Rosie and the machine picked up."

Max moved to the open casement window and lit a cigarette. I stopped my narrative and walked over to the answer machine and pressed play.

> **#1:** "Hi Allyson, it's Rosie. I'm sorry I haven't got in touch with you for a while. Thanks for letting me know about the April 29th meeting, I'm sure I can make it. Also tomorrow I'll be in Stockton. My mom just got back from Japan and I'm down here for the week-end. I'll be home Sunday afternoon so I'm pretty sure that your message said Saturday. Good luck on the test. Let me know how the test went. And how you did. Let me know how things go and if there's anything going on this week."

#2: *A man's voice, I thought to myself, who is this?* "She wore her long brown hair in a braid, rich from the smell of coffee from the café down from her house. It was Saturday evening. She was nowhere to be found, probably playing records, just like the sounds produced by her answer machine. (Laughing at himself.) Tomorrow was an exam. She needed a ride. She was as desperate as a beetle on its back, with its legs struggling in the air…what a metaphor, what an awful metaphor, anyway, (laughing.) I just got back, call me 695-????. He left his message as quick as he left his clandestine lover."

She hadn't told me that she had a new boyfriend. His voice was sexy.

#3: "Hi, Allyson, this is Sonja, it's nine o'clock. I'll be going to bed shortly, so call me in the morning. I should be up about 8 o'clock. Good-bye."

I turned off the playback. "She must have died before nine o'clock Saturday night, so she actually died on April 20. That's good because the 21st is Lawton's birthday. Who was that guy on the machine?"

Rosa said, "I don't know. She didn't mention him when she came to see me last week. Perhaps it was that Scott guy? What an image. 'A bug on its back?' It's almost like he picked up on her struggles for air."

Max spoke, leaning his back against the windowsill. Arms hugging himself, he put together a long string of words in his East Texas accent. "The police found the address book and called my dad in Tyler on Sunday about noon. He wasn't home. He was out with Sarah celebrating his birthday. Gordon, that's his stepson, answered, and the officer asked to speak to Lawton Bennett. Gordon had instructs never to give out information on the phone. He said, 'I can't tell you.'

"'Listen, young man, you have to tell me. This is an emergency from San Francisco.'

"But Gordon stubbornly refused.

"The police called Holly's house. (Max's daughter lived with Nancy's mother, the other grandmother, named Billie Perkins.) Billie said, 'What's this all about? What's happened?'

"So the police told her that Allyson had been found dead in her apartment and they needed to call her parents. Billie gave the police your name, told them Celeste Rose in Eugene. It's really weird because when Dad and Sarah got home they didn't know what happened. Gordon said it was the police from San Francisco. Dad called Allyson's house but just got the machine. They were having friends over for birthday cake and they took the glass-topped table out the French doors and onto the patio. They set the table out there and Dad went in for chairs. Sarah went to get a tray of plates and forks then, Dad and Sarah heard this loud crash. When they looked they saw that the glass top of the table had split diagonally lengthwise."

Max stopped talking and I thought, *That was the dining table that I had bought when we were married, when we were a family of four: Mom and Dad, a son and a daughter. The dining room table where we ate--Sunday breakfast, evening meals and a series of birthday celebrations with our hats and horns. Now the family was severed: by divorce, a stroke hitting Lawton, mental illness afflicting Max's wife Nancy, our grand- daughter living with the other grandparents, and now Allyson has died.*

Max finished his story, "The family table had broken in two like a stroke of lightning."

Winston went into the bathroom. Rosa and I folded out the futon, making it into a bed, Max went into the closet and found sheets and blankets, Winston came out and flipped the foam-rubber-block chair, making it into a narrow bed. Max slept on the floor. We turned off the overhead light; I put on my nightgown that somehow got packed into my carry-on.

The lights inside the apartment went out but it was not dark. The street lights shown through the breeze-blown lace curtains, making beauteous patterns on the wall—big city noises came through the open casement, cars, trucks, motorcycles, people walking or shouting across the streets to one another. A deranged street person yelled something like, "What's it all about anyway? Who the freak knows? No freaking idea. No freaking way. It's all stinking garbage, not some Houdini in a bottle."

As I cuddled up to Rosa on the futon, I thought to myself, *probably Allyson would have known that street person. She used to engage these kinds of people in conversation. She was generous with her time, generous with her caring.* I let myself cry, letting the tears flow down, letting my nose run. Rosa turned to me, holding me. "Sweetheart," she said, "oh, sweetheart, it's such a sad thing. Allyson was our darling."

I don't know if I said it out loud. I felt like I screamed it. "How am I supposed to say good-bye to her? How am I supposed to leave her body in a refrigerator for a week waiting for cremation? Am I supposed to never see her again? Am I supposed to ignore the fact that she is in a cold drawer in some mortuary while we lie here on her bed?"

Then it got quiet. Winston's breathing sounded like he was asleep. I told myself, *Well, I may not sleep, but maybe I can rest.*

I drifted into a waking dream and with it came an answer to my question. *What am I supposed to do, leave her in a cold drawer in a mortuary?*

I had a vision: A frozen scene appeared to me of white mountains surrounding an ice-blue lake, icebergs floating in the water. The sky was pale. In the foreground, in the shallows, floated a gray and white birchbark canoe carrying Allyson's still figure draped in white, her strangely exotic face discolored from the suffocation, her hands holding the orchids and the Buddhist prayer beads, her long henna hair hanging down over the stern of the boat. I entered the dream, my silver hair brushed and left long, wearing pale gray pants and shirt. I moved over to the canoe and, taking my two hands, I pushed the boat. I stood still to watch. Making no sound, the vessel drifted away across the icy water, heading toward the far shore, a place I could not go. It moved slowly and serenely, carrying Allyson away.

It was finished. She was on her own. Parents need to let go of their adult children giving them space to find their own way. Her journey across this lake would last seven days and she had to make the crossing alone. I had asked the question, How can I leave her there in the cold storage at the mortuary?" I needed to know what to do. God heard my cry and the answer came in this dream/vision. I thought, *It is cold, it is beautiful, and she is on a new journey, but not by herself. I had to believe that God was with her and that God was also here with me.*

Another crazy drunk man screamed from the city street. "You think God loves you? That's crap. That's shit. God only is interested in this weird experiment. We're a God-damned ant farm. He sits above and pokes us with little pointy sticks like a stinking chimpanzee." The drunk man walked along, screaming curses from one end of the block to the other.

The phone rang. It was the middle of the night. Max picked up, suspecting that it would be his mentally ill wife, Nancy, from Texas. She was afraid and Max tried to calm her, using a quiet voice in the corner of the room. Nancy was upset and spoke loudly; we all could hear what she said. "Julian keeps calling me, Max. He's harassing me." Max murmured something to comfort her. "He's dangerous, Max. We don't know what he's capable of. He walks by in front of the house, on the street, and yells obscenities at me." Max tried to change the subject. "I'll be home in a couple of days. My mom needs me. My dad. We're all together, and it's really sad, Nancy." They talked about the viewing and about Allyson's death. On and on they talked. Nancy did not want Max to hang up.

This was my second night of torment. Sometimes in the daytime, distractions helped to hide the cruel facts. Incredibly, several seconds would go by and I would forget that Allyson was dead. But at night, the death was all around me and inside me. The nights were hell, but this night Rosa was with me.

Chapter Six

Tuesday, Cleaning the Apartment

Tuesday morning I ate the granola that I had brought with me and milk that Uncle Lynn had bought. Rosa left the apartment to go to her job, promising to return in the early afternoon. Lawton and his crew arrived and we went to work according to plan:

1. Inventory Allyson's belongings.
2. Decide what to do with them.
3. Clean the apartment.
4. Empty the apartment.
5. Move her out.

We had done this before, at the end of her four years of college when we had helped to move her out of her dorm room and into a temporary storage unit.

I was in charge of being in charge. I am a theatre director by trade and I know how to "strike the set." I knew what to do. Besides, I had God and Allyson with me, and the three of us made a good committee for answering questions. What do we do? I worked fast and ruthlessly. I really wanted to get rid of everything. I wanted to get rid of the hurt and agony of going through my daughter's things.

Winston and Max carried bags of trash to the apartment dumpster. Lawton was still recovering from a stroke and he was still somewhat disabled, so he got busy going through books, files and papers, sitting on the floor by the bay window. Aunt Jan and Sarah made an assault on the kitchen, first washing Allyson's pile of dirty dishes and straightening the clutter on the counters.

Winston scoured the dreaded bathroom where Allyson had died. Sarah moved to the closet to go through Allyson's clothes and jewelry. Max worked on his sister's considerable music collection. *Where was her flute?* I know that she had repeatedly pawned it when she was a struggling underemployed person. *Where was her filmscript that she was currently working on?* The briefcase that contained her script was not here.

I picked up a large art-framed poster and put it in the give-away pile. My brother snatched it back and stacked it with the "keep for Celeste" selections. It was a print of Amado Maurillo Pena's work advertising an International Art Expo in New York, 1983. At Mills College, Allyson had taken out a $50 emergency student loan because buying this piece had seemed to her an absolute necessity. The graphic is of an old Indian woman holding a pottery vessel with ancient writings on it. Today I treasure this art piece and display it prominently in my living room.

Brother Winston went out into the world, gathering empty boxes for packing, and bringing in food for us. We made categories and piles of things: a pile for Max and his daughter Holly to be mailed to them by Lynn and Jan; a pile for me and my brother Winston; a pile for Lawton to be mailed to Tyler, Texas; a pile of large things to be kept at Sonja's until I could drive down later to pick them up: Allyson's large trunk with the velvet comforter, her costume collection, some of her original paintings, and her large art pieces.

Allyson had had plans of a future relationship with Holly. The Bennett clan had been together over Christmas in 1990 in Tyler, Texas. Now Allyson's plans were ended. Max and I prepared a gift box for Holly. Using one of Allyson's baskets, the one that looked like a pirate's treasure box, we loaded it with great grandma's dresser set, four china tea cups and saucers, several vampire books, framed photos and a quorum of stuffed animals including a two-foot-tall Sasquatch. Uncle Lynn included this collection to be mailed to Holly at a later date.

Snap decisions: give the futon and the furniture to the friend who was just getting her new apartment; give Allyson's clothes to the Buddhist temple friends and let them keep what they want and take the rest to Goodwill. Keep family heirlooms: books, journals, and papers, photo albums, one special plate for me, earrings for Sarah, jewelry for anyone who liked. There was a precious little black-gold ring with a heart-shaped garnet that I immediately put on my left pinkie finger. I selected faux cinnabar earrings, pink quartz earrings, and a golden brooch in the shape of a mask.

Clyde came knocking on the door. He had been Allyson's boss when she was down and out. She worked at his coffee store here in the Mission District. Clyde was a short, stocky man with thick hair on his head and hairy arms. He was crying and talking.
"I can't believe it! Oh, no. No one believes it!"

"It was the epilepsy. She suffocated during a seizure."

"Oh God, no. I'm so sorry. If you need anything, call me. Everyone come down to the store and we'll have a cup of coffee."

At noon we left the apartment to go to a Mexican restaurant for lunch. It was good to be out-of-doors in the sun and walking. Again, festivity gathered around food, with laughter and tears. I walked with my ex-husband, Lawton. I could see how the stroke had affected his stride and his speech. We talked about our former family and how we had raised our kids. We had regrets. I had regrets.

He said, "We did the best we could."

We put some items on the sidewalk downstairs with a sign saying "FREE". As we walked away we heard voices approaching the "free" pile. "Look at this, a computer! Come here, over here, look at this." When we came back from the Mexican lunch everything that was on the street had disappeared except for what Rosa called the "naughty bits." I remember her saying, "It's like a meal of fish, they ate the meat and left the bones." Remaining on the sidewalk were various pairs of panties, wire coat-hangers, a torn poster, a can of spinach, an open box of tampons, and a worn paperback book entitled *Ten Strategies to a Better Life*. The book had not mentioned death. Death was not one of the strategies, at least not on this earthly plane.

Larry arrived, bringing roses that he had grown in his back yard. "Imagine, there behind my apartment is an abandoned rose bush! I tended it and made the roses bloom." He was crying. He promised to come back tomorrow to help distribute some of Allyson's belongings.   He wanted her file cabinet and Allyson's movie equipment. We gladly gave these things to him.

*   *   *

Allyson had been studying movie-making. It was her future career, her passion. She began at Mills College with film classes and worked in the TV lab there. Her films were dark in subject.

She had always had dark dreams. As a tiny child she dreamed of monsters and large insects. *Was the epilepsy there in her mind even then, causing the shadowy images?*

Her first seizure that we knew about had been in the spring of her senior year at Churchill High School. She had been working on the music computer, and when she walked into the breezeway she had fallen violently to the cement. The principal called me.

I said, "I will be there in an hour."

She said, "Come now."

I walked into the nurse's room. Allyson lay on a cot with a shockingly white face and dark circles under her eyes. I asked, "What is it?"

The nurse responded, "Does Allyson use drugs?"

"I don't think so."

"She had a seizure outside the music room."

I thought the worst first: *Maybe it's a brain tumor.* David King, my high-school friend, had died in our senior year from a brain tumor.

Allyson was conscious but confused and distressed. We walked to the green and blue polka dot puppet van that we used for a car and drove her directly to Uncle Winston's medical office, an internist, he looked her over and sent us to the neurologist. After she was examined with an E.K.G. machine, we waited. By the end of the day we walked into the brain doctor's office and were told, "She has epilepsy."

I sighed with relief. Allyson was relieved also. *Oh, we can deal with that, a few pills and she'll be just fine. I like this diagnosis. It could be worse.*

She began with Phenobarbital, which is inexpensive and easy to administer. Her second seizure was a month later on the morning of her graduation day. Rosa was in her room, I was in the living room, and Allyson was using the hair dryer. *Had the roar of the hair dryer been a trigger?* We heard a loud crash.

Allyson was on the floor doing her gentle rocking and mild kind of thrashing. It was the first time that I had seen her in this condition, with eyes rolled back and slobbering at the mouth. I crawled on the floor to her and held her loosely, protecting her from the wall and the bathroom fixtures.

Rosa came in. "Oh, Allyson," she said, "Easy, easy, it's OK." We tended her.

After the seizure Allyson seemed spacey, lost in limbo-land. She did not know what day it was or what, if anything, had happened, but then within an hour she was fine and by the end of the day she attended graduation and the celebratory parties with no complications.

Had there been other seizures that we didn't know about? The time when as a junior-high-age person, she woke up crying and confused. She had spilled water in her bed, or had she wet the bed? There were times when I heard bumping from her bed on the bedroom wall and thought that she might have been masturbating. But had that been a seizure? Perhaps she had *petit-mals* when she dropped a glass for no reason, shards and liquid contents spraying out over the kitchen. The times she forgot what she was saying in mid-sentence. Or perhaps she had jerked her head or twitched her hand. How long had she had the epilepsy? Were the grand-mal seizures brought on by a reaction to Nutra-Sweet? Allyson drank a lot of diet Pepsi, gallons per week.

She began her daily medication for seizure control when she was just graduating from high school. She wanted me to stay out of it and not ask questions. So as a parent, I was never involved in her epilepsy management. She went to Mills College at the end of August where she worked with the infirmary and a local Oakland neurologist for her medication. I understood that if a person takes too large a dose, there are no seizures, but the quality of life is affected. Life would become bland, losing the dramatic edge. If you undermedicate, then you have occasional seizures, which are frighteningly dangerous. The main dangers are head injuries, suffocation or accidents. Control of this condition is very like handling a tarantula, continuing your daily life while keeping a careful eye on the hairy monster.

She told me that she had seizures once a month, a seeming connection with her menstrual cycle, but sometimes going several months without incidents. Seizures were embarrassing. The overreaction of the witnesses was problematic. Seeing her, the witnesses would immediately call the medics, but an ambulance ride at that time cost over $900.00. Fortunately, she was still on her father's health insurance plan, but she still became frustrated.

"I don't need medics. I just need to be protected for one or two minutes." When I watched the seizures they always seemed very long, and then she needed a quiet time afterwards to pull herself back together.

Once she had a seizure at the end of a jazz dance class. Another time, when she was directing a Greek drama, she seized in front of her student-actors. They called the medics. Once, alone in the dorm, she had gone to the laundry room and "come to" in her room; she couldn't find her books or her glasses because her things were all on the washing machine; after the seizure, she had been wandering around the building in a state of confusion.

One time on the phone I asked, "Do you have any warning? Why don't you sit down until it's over?"

"I do! I sit there and wait and then just before it hits, I think, oh it's over and I get up to go on with what I'm doing and then I black out. It's very tricky."

After a long conversation, I said the un-sayable. "This could kill you."

She answered low, "Yes, I know."

She told me about adventurous seizures, like the one with the punk band. Allyson was living in San Francisco and had gone to an illegal drinking and dancing party. The party-goers attending wore white make-up with spiked hair, leather clothes, and chains. People were dancing and drinking. The police entered the venue through the back door and began to arrest the people in charge and to question the dancers.

The word went around, "Tell people that the beer is free and that this is just a party."

Allyson didn't drink alcohol because of her medical condition but she definitely liked dancing and shaking her head. Had the trigger been, again, the loud music? In the middle of the raid, Allyson fell violently to the floor and had a seizure. She opened her eyes and looking down at her was a man with a white painted face and pink hair. He said, "What do you need? I'm a medic."

Allyson looked around, frightened. "Get me out of here! Don't call for an ambulance, please. It's just epilepsy." Two punks helped her up and led her out of a side door. One of the band members sat with her at a coffee shop until she recovered.

A romantic seizure. Once at Mills College she was sitting with two male professors at the cafeteria. She had a seizure while sitting in a chair. One handsome professor knelt to her right and the other to her left. They talked to her and comforted her until she stabilized. "Mom, it was so neat. One guy is my German professor. He knelt beside me and gazed into my eyes and stroked my hair."

Another time, it was right after Larry's ex-wife had talked to him on the telephone. She was a lady who acted crazy. One time she threw his TV out of his window, and she often screamed at him. This may have been a stress trigger for Allyson. When he was on the phone with his wife and she was giving him a hard time, Allyson "passed out." She woke up with Larry lying beside her holding her in his arms.

Julius Caesar had epilepsy and the word "seizure" comes from him. Other famous people who suffered from the disorder were Tchaikovsky, Napoleon, and poor Edward Lear, who had several seizures a day. He called it his demon and often drew pictures of himself with the devil on his shoulder.

During the summer at Uncle Farley's house, Aunt Mary, an RN, had heard Allyson hit the floor in a seizure. When she told me about it, she had a tone of disgust about the incident. After that I always felt that Aunt Mary believed that epilepsy was somehow shameful. It was awful all right, but it wasn't shameful to me. My darling daughter could do nothing shameful.

Once at Christmas at Uncle Farley's, Allyson was feeling unwell and sitting in a kitchen chair when I saw her have a seizure. It was the second one that I personally witnessed. Her cousin Anne, my niece, ran out of the room. I believed it was because she thought that the seizure was "gross," but years later, she said that it was just that she wanted to give us privacy. She didn't want to gawk.

Poor Allyson also had terrifically horrible headaches. I don't think they were migraines as she didn't need to go to bed for twenty-four hours in a darkened room. But her head hurt.

She tried diet control, acupuncture, prayer, meditations, and different medications.

We were both in denial at the beginning. She called her seizures "black outs, passing out, fainting spells," and for her, that's what it was like.

I didn't want to believe that she really had epilepsy, so I carried this denial around with me for a year or two, with her living in California and me in Oregon. She was now an adult and I had to let her make her own medical decisions. For me it was traumatic, having my daughter so far from me while she dealt with this life-threatening disease.

My theatre friend, Jon, and I were sitting in a fast-food joint, and I began to talk about Allyson's epilepsy. The more I talked, the more I shared my deep feelings, the more upset I became until I began to sob uncontrollably. We got out of this public place as quickly as we could. Out in the parking lot I began to scream and cry. "My darling wonderful perfect daughter has a disease and it can't be fixed!" I ran to the back of the building where there was the drive-through and beyond to a chain-link fence. Jon followed. I grabbed hold of the fence and began to push and pull on it. I yelled, "It isn't fair, it isn't fair, oh no not her, not her. I don't want her to have epilepsy. Epilepsy is awful and horrible and I don't want her to have it any more. I am so scared! I want it to stop!"

Jon took his place beside me and he grabbed the fence and began to echo my words. He helped me have my tantrum fit. He worked with two-year-olds and at his pre-school he knew exactly what to do. He screamed. "It isn't fair. Nobody ever ever ever should get epilepsy. Stop, stop making this happen. No, no. I hate epilepsy it's a poo-poo disease, it's a crummy dumb-head icky awful thing. I'm going to punch it and poke it." He beat up on the fence beside me.

I continued crying, now barely able to articulate, just making animal noises, when a man walked up to us and said, "Excuse me, but could you give me a jump start?"

I looked at the guy, snot running out of my nose, "What?"

"My car won't start, I think I have a dead battery. Can you give me a jump start?"

I said, "I'm having a fit right now. I'm very upset and I can't help anyone, please go away." Jon and I went back to what we were doing and the stranger walked away.

Twenty minutes later, we got into my polka dot van and drove around the restaurant. The man with the broken car was sitting there waiting for help with his hood up.

I pulled up and let him use his cables on my car and we jumped his battery. I told him, "My daughter is very sick and I don't think she's going to get well. I'm sorry about the scene over there."

He said, "Oh sure, I understand. It's awful when your kids get sick."

*   *   *

Back in the apartment where we were going through her things-- I went into Allyson's bathroom and opened the medicine cabinet. I took all of her drugs and threw them in the trash. I threw away her toothbrush and her face cream. I saved her make-up, her lipsticks, foundation, eye-shadows. I saved her hairbrush. I stopped to pull henna colored hair out of her brush and wound it into a ball and put it in my pocket. I put her make-up case in one of the large suitcases that we had brought. I put in her teddy bear, who our Italian friend Franka had named Sympatico; I included her rubber snake, an afghan that grandma, my mother, had made and her aqua-colored, warm and comfy bathrobe. I was packing as if I could make her well, as if I were preparing a bag to take to the hospital. If I could find her and give her her teddy bear and her afghan then she would get well.

       *   *   *

I supported her self-care for her condition. I understood that she didn't want to over-medicate and become a zombie. She was lively. She wanted to live life fully. She had to walk the line of just enough medication to keep seizures from happening, but sometimes her medication would need adjusting.

After my burger-joint fit on the chain link fence, I realized that I had been in the first two stages of dealing with Allyson's disease, Step One in this case being "Shock" which includes Denial.

Pulling my chin over the wall, my eyes peered into the land of the Seven Steps to Recovery with, far away on the horizon, being Step Seven "Acceptance." I determined that I would become educated on epilepsy. That same week I went to Sacred Heart Hospital and used the medical library, as anyone can. I spent the entire afternoon curled up in a comfortable chair with a whole stack of seizure disorder books. I particularly liked the books that interviewed the patients themselves and how they had learned to live with the disorder. Most people with epilepsy make small medication decisions for themselves, but at frequent intervals, they need to have their blood level checked by their Neurologists for chemical percentages. After this research, I talked to Allyson with some new knowledge and passed on what might be useful. Specifically how other people lived with epilepsy. It is a closet disease and many who have it, keep it secret.

From what I understand, people with seizure disorders develop their own rules to live by.

1. Lie. Never tell the truth on job applications or drivers license because there is discrimination against people with epilepsy. Common sense is applied to driving. Allyson was a big-city woman, so she didn't own a car, but she kept an Oregon drivers license just in case.

2. You lie to get the job. After you are safely employed, then you slowly and gently introduce the fact that you

have epilepsy and that it is controlled and not a problem. But if a seizure should occur, keep the area safe and do not call the medics.

3. Dating. Don't tell. But the very moment when you think that this person is a possible life-mate, then immediately tell about your condition. Then if they run away, it is before you are heavily involved.

There are all kinds of seizures. My friend in Eugene had the kind where she'd begin to scribble on paper and use foul language, almost like Tourette's Syndrome. Another person may fall down and thrash violently. (People no longer are to put pencils in anyone's mouth. Bad idea.)

The suffocation deaths I've heard about are one old man who rolled off the couch and smothered himself in a pillow; children smothered while asleep in their beds at night; a young woman drowned in her bathtub.

*   *   *

Rosa and Sarah were cleaning Allyson's closet. We discovered that she had a considerable collection of thick wool too-large coats and men's too-large trench coats. She had black lace stretch leggings and blouses that she wore with her black mini skirts —this she called "San Francisco vogue." We found Larry's old black leather jacket with the chains and multiple zippers on it. Because he now worked for U.P.S., his shoulder and arm muscles had bulked up and he could no longer fit into his leather jacket. We decided to give it to Max's wife, Nancy, who is quite slender. Max took the journalist's vest, a tan colored canvas vest with 14 pockets. In the trunk by the bay window she had collected several costume items, like her Spanish-looking red prom dress, her cap and gown from Mills, her grandmother Phyllis's rhinestone decorated strap heels, and her grandmother Bennett's Chinese dresses.

Rosa and I held up the heavy, too-large coat. We tried to remember when was it that Allyson had protested against the federal testing of nuclear weapons. It was in the middle of a cold winter that she went into the desert. She wore this heavy too-large wool coat and trespassed onto restricted property where she was rounded up with a couple hundred other protesters, cuffed, and taken to jail. She was very proud of this short-lived internment.

She had an independent sense of style. In high school she would sketch out clothing and I would sew for her on my Singer Featherweight machine. She wore these clothes with style and pride.

She and I had managed the transition between parent and child to the mature relationship of two women friends. I managed this by keeping my mouth shut and reacting to communication not always with advice but more as a friend would do. I gave her encouragement and truly enjoyed her company. She also appreciated me. She was one of my life cheerleaders and was proud of having an artistic mom. "Go Mom!"

That dance weekend a year ago I had stayed at her old apartment closer to downtown, but still in the Mission district. I slept in the room with her altar and every morning she came in and chanted her prayers, while I happily lay pretending to sleep. It was like *nirvana* to hear her chanting.

Chapter Seven

Reading her Journals

In her apartment on that April day when we all read pieces from her journals, I was proud that there were no surprises in these pages. I knew my daughter; she and I were intimate friends with current knowledge of one another.

She went all the way through college without losing her virginity, not because of a sense of morality but just because she hadn't had "that" kind of a boyfriend. Graduated from college and living as a single girl in San Francisco, she suddenly got tired of holding on to her virginity. She wanted to get "that" over with.

THE ICE QUEEN USED TO BE ME
AJB: **Journal, age 22**

So Barbara the most amazing night I mean—last Monday was we...it all started when I got locked out of my flat. I came home from work and discovered I'd forgotten my keys. My roommate wasn't home so I went to [the café'] Ground Zero, talked to Laura and had some coffee. Went back by the house still no one home so I went to Sharon's hung out a while. Sharon and I chatted about Thomas, a 17 year old, that I was considering establishing a relationship with but I was unsure because of his age but then Sharon says you might as well get them at their peak. Anyway, that's another story. So I went back by the house, still no one home.

It was about 10:30 p.m. by then and I had my work clothes on carrying around my brief case and I was overwhelmed by the desire to sit and write. So I went to Café Flora.

Once seated, writer's block set in so I started scribbling about Thomas trying to figure out what I really wanted. This guy at a table across from me was checking me out. I did my best to ignore him, the last thing I needed was another man after my ass, feast or famine, you know. He was writing too. I was beginning to think he was writing about me staring at him writing…at 11:00 p.m. he stood up and said, "What are you writing?"

"Oh. just scribbling."

"Yeah, I do that a lot."

"What are you writing?" I asked.

I've forgotten his response. We started chatting. I was cold at first; trying to avoid real interaction. [My Buddhist friend,] Joy says. "You shouldn't talk to strangers." That's gotten me in trouble recently. But, he was really neat. The café' closed. I really should go home. Mrs. Douglas [the landlady] would be home by now and I don't want to wake her too late.

"Do you know any places around here that could still be open, where we could talk?"

"Well, yeah. There's an all night place over on Church St. Sparkey's. Kind of too trendy and bright and obnoxious."

"Then maybe we shouldn't go there."

"Yeah but, it's still open and will stay open."

"OK." So went to Sparky's and talked… …. … Bright guy, grad student in journalism at UCB. He mentioned a place around Polk he liked, The Great Steak, an all-night joint.

"Do you want to go there?"

"I really should go home. I have an appointment at 8:30, also I shouldn't wake my roommate up too late." It's now 2:00 a.m.

"Well, you could stay at my place."

"Okay, let's go." I hopped on the back of his red Vespa. All right what does this mean? So we ate grub-steak then hash browns, and went to his apartment in North Beach-- great place two rooms, a kitchen and a roof.

On the roof we stand. "Look, you can see the ocean, the bay and downtown lights." I wished that he'd touch me. Back inside we sit on the bed and he makes the move.

"Uhh, Marc," he stops and smiles at me, "before you get too excited, I don't have my birth control with me."

"Well, I have condoms. I haven't used them in 4 years but, not too force the issue, but I have them."

"Okay, I'll think about it." Okay, so sometime later we're both naked. "When you're getting pretty close you better get a condom, but you should probably know, I'm a virgin, but I'm getting pretty bored with it."

"Do you want to?"

"Well, I kind a wanted my first to be someone I'd known for more than one night."

"Or three hours?" Then, "Well, I should get a condom on in the heat of passion sometimes it's hard to stop."

"Yeah." At some point I just told him to go for it.

"Tell me if it hurts."

"It's gonna hurt, no escaping that." A little difficulty. "I'm pretty small."

The next hour or so is a dream of pain and passion. I clenched my teeth determined not to scream, but then just gave up, relaxed and let go. Marc brought out the passion in me. I don't know how long, it seemed to be a never ending dream of like I said, pain and passion.

Marc Romero, 15 Nobles. (Alley off Grant on North Beach.)

Finally we curled up together and he slept. I rested but was shaking, I couldn't sleep. I bled a lot.

Fast forward to Thursday. We're back at his place in bed. First we talk about Monday. I say, "Was it okay?"

He says, "It's really great to see someone...be with someone who's so...impassioned." (I forget the word, but it basically meant turned on.)

I told him that I'd had to think about it to figure out how much I liked it. After all, it did hurt a lot. But after wading through the dream of that night, I decided that yes, I had fun! Okay, so I still wasn't sure how much of it was Marc and how much was just sex.

So Saturday night I went to Berkeley for a party, only I had a headache. I had decided earlier that day that I didn't want to sleep with anyone but Marc for a while, only so much I can deal with that early in my sexual life, but...I'd always been attracted to Jeff and it would be interesting to see what someone else was like. My inexperience seems to flash like neon.

He'd given me a Tylenol earlier and when we stopped having sex, my headache was completely gone.

Take 2 Tylenol and get laid.

I don't feel bad about the experience with Jeff, it makes me see and understand more that the way Marc moves me sexually is special. But outside of bed I still am shy and feel uncomfortable with Marc. Strange dichotomy.

Jeff knows about my Monday night experience. His response was two words. "After Hours." And I thought, "Wow." In the movies, time distorts completely. As if night goes on forever, never seems to end, morning will never come and I finally can really relate to that.

"Just think," I say to Jeff. "I met Marc at 11:00 p.m. and by 3:30 a.m. I was in bed with him."

Jeff says, "That's not so bad."

"Yeah, but can you imagine meeting someone at 11:00 in the morning and being in bed with them by 3:30 that afternoon?" Silence. "Time totally distorts in the hours between midnight and daylight."

Jeff says, "How do we deal with it?"

I say, "We sleep."

So back to Barbara. In Ground Zero on Friday, I told her parts of this story, leaving out my virginity and after I'd established some trust, I said, in a low voice. "You know before Monday night I was a virgin."

Her eyes widened, "Your head must be spinning!"

"Yeah." I guess you could say that.

Then later she told me this story. In Boston a woman-friend on Beacon Hill lived with a man. Their relationship was great, no visible tension and things hadn't gotten dull, mundane, stagnate. One day he was gone, without a word, no note, no trace, no explanation whatsoever. He left her apartment, took his things and was gone.

So she decided to take a break from men for a while, think about things, get over this desertion. A year and a half later the men on Beacon Hill had dubbed her the Ice Queen. She had style, she didn't let it bother her. She laughed and said, "Yeah, I know, I'm the Ice Queen."

Barbara has left me and I am writing, scribbling…I used to be the Ice Queen, 22 years of celibacy and when age 21 came around, I had started to worry, am I sexless? I began chipping away at the wall around myself but it took a while. Just before my 22nd birthday I came just short of having sex with a guy on the hippy bus called The Green Tortoise on my way home to Oregon for Christmas. Isaac Arnett, going to his island off the Washington coast to live in a camper. I thought about having sex with him, but I knew I'd bleed and scream and that would be un-cool, with people sleeping right next to us on either side. So I used the no birth control excuse. He said he had a vasectomy. I pretended not to believe him. "Yeah, that's what they all say."

He commented on how sad it is we live in a society where people can't trust each other. I pretended to fall asleep and he jacked off on my leg.

Then there was David Mason at Mills. We played around some but…the night I had a chance, I didn't feel comfortable telling him that I was a virgin, so I didn't. Then he never tried again. Persistence would have gotten him somewhere but he was seeing this weird Nina woman, and I think he felt uncomfortable with sleeping with both of us, as much as he wanted to.

So I graduated, moved to S.F. and all of a sudden all these men think I'm beautiful. At first I thought it was because, through being broke I'd starved myself to thinness…more then before. I do look thin, but Sarah says it's that I look more relaxed then she'd ever seen me. I guess at school the tension was written all over me, though I don't remember it having such a visible effect, but I guess it did.

So all of a sudden I'm beautiful and all these men are interested in me. I didn't know how to deal with it. The first step is the hardest. Everyone said, "When you least expect it…"

And then Thomas, but that was too set up and Thomas is very intelligent but something wasn't there. We came close to doing it but I don't know, I used the birth control excuse again.

So I'd have time to think about him and the midst of thinking about him, Marc appeared and--THE ICE QUEEN MELTED--So it's Sunday night or rather Monday morning, 1:30 a.m., in Orphan Andy's, I came here out of frustration.   Went out with Marc to a monologue by Spalding Gray. I expected to stay with him tonight, even took my work clothes with me.   But he had three reviews to write by noon tomorrow.

OK, I get the picture. He took me home, had one night with me and now I'm turning into nymphomaniac? Last week at this time I was a virgin, but knowing, IT WILL BE SOON. So I sit smoking, drinking coffee, writing, [birth control] sponge still in place. Barbara says, "Just be careful, you don't want to turn a good experience into a bad one."

"Yeah, I bought my sponges, I'm going to be careful really." Living from date to date but thrilled.   COLLECTING LIFE EXPERIENCE THE ICE QUEEN HAS MELTED, YEAH! But I still need to sleep, better go home to bed.

So once upon a time there was an ice princess who lived on Beacon Hill...She lived happily with a man and one day he disappeared. She went out with someone else soon afterward, but she was paranoid. She read into meaningless events that he was going to leave her, so one night they went, in her car, to a movie. She dropped him to buy the tickets, saying that she'd park the car but she never came back. He paced back and forth in front of the theatre for three hours.

Some time later, after a year and a half of celibacy, she went for a walk with a male friend. As they sat talking on a bridge over some railroad tracks, he tried to kiss her. She pushed him away and in so doing started to fall over the railing. He tried to catch her and in so doing they both fell to their deaths.

Chapter Eight

Living in San Francisco

At one point that year Allyson had run into a string of bad luck with roommates. One of them had skipped out with the rent money leaving them two months behind. Then the next roommate did not stay and had paid her nothing. There she was with a minimum-wage job and a huge rent payment due, so Allyson went to an exotic dance parlor, The Lusty Lady and got a job, nights and week-ends. I called this job being a "Hootchy kootchy dancer." There she wore scanty costumes over her nude body, such as a small cowboy vest on top and on the bottom leather chaps with nothing underneath. On other days she wore a Japanese kimono and danced in such a way that her nude body could be easily seen. She told me that one night she dressed as a graduating student wearing her black gown over her naked body with the front unzipped and her mortar board hat. If the Mills College Dean of Women could see her now!

When she called me in Eugene and told me her solution to her money problems, I reacted with a hysterical outburst.

She said, "Mom, when I mentioned it before, you laughed."

"It must have been nervous laughter, because I don't think that it's funny."

I felt that she would lose forever a certain trust in life and that she could never regain her innocence. I worried that she'd become cynical and hardened. I grieved for her lost purity, but I was in Eugene and she was in San Francisco, so I tried to keep my feelings to myself. There, her Buddhist women advisors counseled against her working as a nude dancer. But Allyson made lots of money and began to pay off her out-of-control bills. The Lusty Lady liked her imaginative costumes and her dancing and they gave her a raise every week. Allyson justified this work by calling it "research for future writing projects." She spent some of the time at the dance parlor interviewing the other dancers about their lives and their philosophies. She was able to quit after six weeks.

What I remember is, she said that the men had private viewing rooms and she could see them masturbating, always with their ties flung back; that ever after that she was suspicious of men with their ties hanging over one shoulder. Later, after her death, I said to myself, that if she was going to have a short life, maybe she needed to have as many sexual adventures as she could.

I felt pride that I had raised a daughter who was comfortable with her body. She was beautiful--short, with rounded hips, a slim waist, and full firm breasts. She was a good dancer. When I write down her description I say: A dancer, a writer, a good friend, intelligent, talkative, messy in her house, did not take care of her clothes, smoked too much, had an irritating habit of cracking her wrist joints, also spiritual, loving, a painter, an optimist with a good sense of humor, responsible for her own bills, reliable. Her dark humor showed in her poetry and her films.

                    *   *   *

Tuesday night there was a potluck dinner and a memorial service at the home of Allyson's Buddhist chief. The place was past San Francisco University, with a view of winding avenues, palm trees, and colorful hill top houses like cup cakes on a pastry shelf. Inside the door there was an area for people to remove their shoes. I met Allyson's other Buddhist friends, some of her movie-making cohorts and was thrilled and delighted to greet again her California cousins, Mike and Kelly, Uncle Lynn's children, all grown up and beautiful.

I met Allyson's friend Karen Red-Green whom I had heard so much about through the years. She is small and tough, a mannish-looking woman, who wore a New York Yankees cap with the brim cut off. She had scraggly teeth and a rough voice. This week I had heard her voice on Allyson's last answer machine tape.

Allyson had been the maid-of-honor when Karen decided to marry herself at Golden Gate Park. The date was 8-8-88 at 8:00 a.m. The 8:00 a.m. part seemed to be a good idea but Karen was not a morning person. It was Allyson's job to wake her on that day and get her to the park on time.

Her original name was Karen Red and she had made many films in which she talked and argued with her other self, Karen Green. On 8-8-88 she married herself and became Karen Red-Green.

At the Buddhist memorial, people stood with paper plates and forks eating the potluck dinner and mingling. I was dressed in a purple easy fitting dress and wore the dusty rose-colored opera coat that Allyson had given me. Every once in a while, Allyson would splurge and buy me expensive presents. I enjoyed wearing the beautiful coat. I also carried a large handkerchief. Everyone at the gathering alternated between laughing and crying.

Allyson's friends told me stories. Carol, the young Buddhist friend from last night, told me that once she and Allyson were walking down the street in the Mission District. They began to talk about pizza. Allyson and Carol started to skip along the sidewalk. They imagined that they were eating pieces of stringy pizza, pantomiming the droopy slices. Everyone who passed them smiled and said, "Pizza!" A bus driver stopped and leaned out his window and said, "Pizza!" A young black guy wearing a stocking cap said, "Pizza!" The mother with the baby stroller said, "Pizza!" Allyson and Carol twirled and danced eating their imaginary slices. It was like a scene from a Gene Kelly and Debbie Reynolds movie, only it wasn't Paris and it wasn't raining, it was sunny San Francisco on Mission Blvd., and they were eating imaginary pizza.

The living room was full of people. There were rows of folding chairs. I sat by the window in the second row. The Buddhists began to chant, pressing their hands together and rattling their prayer beads. The owner of the house was somewhat wealthy, an American of Chinese descent, and the front wall of the room was covered with a large elaborate altar, floor to ceiling. The wood, decorated with red lacquer, was inlaid with flowers and birds made from mother-of-pearl. There were doors and hinges operated by electrical buttons. Pillared niches contained vases with flowers, bowls of fruit offerings, and trays of burning incense. The altar was illuminated with tiny built-in spotlights. The room began to collect clouds of fragrant smoke. The Buddhists among us chanted. The only part I recognized was the Devotion to the Lotus Sutra, *nam myoho renge kyo*. The room reverberated with the sound of many voices. The tones and semi-tones and unsung harmonics blended into exotic chords, including the rumble of sub-bass sounds. Against the wooden chair, my bones vibrated with the prayers. I began to relax into the tones surrounded by fragrant smoke. I felt floaty, with feelings of an out-of-body experience, similar to those achieved from Gabriel Roth and her authentic movement class.

One leader invited people to speak. Allyson's Uncle Winston stood and spoke, then her friends, her Buddhist teachers, her Dad spoke, and I spoke. I didn't cry, I spoke out like the performer that I am. "I thought that I would come to San Francisco alone to take care of Allyson, her body and her belongings. I thought that I would drive here alone with my car and a trailer and clean her messy apartment." The people laughed; the running joke of Allyson and her messy apartment was well known. "But incredibly, I have not been alone. From the beginning I have been supported by my family, by Allyson's friends and by God. I so appreciate the Buddhist religion and the feeling of support of these your chants and prayers. I am here to testify that I am proud of Allyson, she was a wonderful daughter. In the last year, as most of you know, she prayed earnestly for peace on the planet Earth. I am glad that she lived to see the Berlin Wall come down, that she saw the end of the Gulf War. Thank you, Allyson, for being my daughter."

Winston, Max, Rosa, and I spent Tuesday night, a second and last night, at the apartment.

Chapter Nine

Wednesday, "It is Finished."

On Wednesday morning, son Max and Uncle Winston, traveling by BART and bus, went on a four-hour tour of San Francisco, taking Allyson's camera with them. Max was excited, he had been living a life of poverty in Texarkana, Texas, and had not seen much of the world. Rosa went to work. I was now alone and very glad to be. I had been with people all of Monday and all of Tuesday. *Was it only such a short time?* I sat on the foam chair. The stacked objects of Allyson's home stood around me, sorted belongings, all assigned to go to different people and places.

Sonja came with a helper to take the large things that I wanted to keep. She planned to save them at her house until I could drive down: the costume trunk, brass music stand, two folding leather butterfly chairs, the large painting, and the bookshelf music system.

Sonja knelt by my chair touching my arm and looking into my face. She said, "We were so afraid when we were at the community center and Allyson didn't arrive for the test. We knew something was wrong. We phoned in the night and in the morning but we got no response. Celeste, you know, I told you, that I'm a welfare cop by profession and I've had experience in breaking into apartments, searching the premises. I was so afraid when we came in, the place was so warm, so awful hot. I told you before, I'm the one who found Allyson's body. I knew she was dead and probably from epilepsy but we had to call the police anyway. She was a wonderful person. We're all so sad to say good-bye."

I said, "Thank you, Sonja, I'm happy that you were the one to find her. You did the right thing to get into the apartment and find her."

Allyson's friend Carol, from the coffee shop, was moving into a new apartment and needed furniture. She and her crew came next with her friend's telephone truck. They carried out the futon couch, tables and chairs and bookshelves.

Larry came with his pickup truck for the filing cabinet and things that he owned with Allyson. As agreed, he took all of the movie equipment. He said, "I'll be back at four o'clock to take you to the airport. Allyson always said you were a great mom. I'm really glad to at last meet you."

Candice came. She too knelt beside my chair and touched my arm. It was like these people came at their assigned times to kneel and give me honor as they took away Allyson's belongings, emptying the apartment.

Candice told me this story, "Allyson was friends with Anna, my 18-month-old daughter. She had given Anna a picture book, *The Polka Dot Bear*. Every time she visited, Allyson played with my daughter and read the book to her. This week when I cried and acted sad about Allyson's death, my little girl came to me and said, 'Mommy, crying?' I said, 'Allyson, our friend, has gone away and will never come back. It makes me very sad to tell her good-bye.' Anna toddled over to the bookshelf, pulled out *The Polka Dot Bear*, put it in my lap and patted my arm." Here in Allyson's apartment Candice looked into my eyes, "Imagine a child so young, recognizing Allyson's name, remembering the book and trying to console me."

I reached to touch her hair, "It is a sweet story, thank you."

Candice said, "Tell me what to do. I want to help you."

I said, "Please would you wash the bathroom again. That's where Allyson died and I'd like it to be scrubbed with bleach. We already cleaned it but you know, it still doesn't seem clean." She quietly sanitized the room again and in a little while she was gone.

The apartment was being cleared out.

Janet came and transported all the bags of clothing to the Buddhist center and the Goodwill. "Please," I said, "Find someone who knows Allyson to wear her new boots. She was so thrilled to get them. I think her new boots were the last things she thought about. The things she regretted leaving the most."

"I promise," said Janet.

Newlywed friend Denise came. The last time she saw Allyson was at her and Albert's wedding. She picked out dishes and the brand new blender and the coffee making supplies. She took a vase from Allyson's altar.

Sonja came back to get Allyson's newly-paid-for *gohonzon* so that she could give it to Allyson's Buddhist student, a young single mother who lived in the Mission District. Also some of Allyson's clothes would fit her. Allyson's brother, Max, was taking her old altar to his house in Texas, along with a few items for Nancy and Holly. Rosa took some of Allyson's art supplies, several blank canvases and brushes. Sarah, Allyson's stepmother, was also taking art supplies and some jewelry.

All this time, between visits from Allyson's friends, I sat alone in the foam chair, thinking about all that had happened. I held the stories that people told me close to my heart, the last remaining tales of Allyson's young life. In my pocket I had a lock of her hair that I had taken from the hairbrush. I twisted it and pulled it, rolling it in my fingers. I'd like to hang on to what was left and never let it go.

Tony came, a gay photographer friend who had loaned Allyson the beautiful lace curtains for her bay windows. He climbed up on the window ledge and, using a broom, he managed to bring the curtain rods down so that he could retrieve the curtains. He folded them and talked. He brought me pictures of Allyson and a picture of a beautiful creamy-white lotus flower.

Tony sat on the floor beside my chair and told me this story. He held his hands closed tight and close to his body and he said, "The lotus flower grows from below in the mud. Under the mud it is dark, close, no sun, no air, yet in all the darkness there is the promise of life surviving within the roots of the plant. The darkness is part of the flower. The darkness is part of the beauty." His hand rose up, illustrating the opening of the lotus. "When the precious flower breaks up through ground, it opens to the sun, and reaching to the sky, it feels the touch of the warm breeze. This is the essence of what

Nam myoho renge kyo means. Even when the flower is gone, the lotus is still there, waiting underground."

I thought, *my daughter is like a lotus blossom.* Later, at home in Eugene, when it was too painful to have pictures of Allyson around my room and I had hidden all of her pictures away, I had Tony's photograph of the lotus flower out on the shelf. *This is my daughter,* I would say*, she's changed;* and remembering the new colors of her body, I saw how like an orchid she had become.

Jennifer wanted Allyson's antique wicker-bottomed wheelchair. I didn't tell her that it was cursed. Whoever owns this chair will die an untimely death. Jennifer also took the large *fica* tree and the other houseplants. There was a small bear with clamping arms in the *fica* tree. "Oh, here's your bear," Jennifer said.

I smiled, "No, the bear goes with the tree."

Jennifer took the large white sculpture-head. This was the scene: Jennifer pushed the antique wheelchair down Capp Street, turned onto 24th Street and crossed Mission. In the chair was the *fica* tree, various other houseplants, and a large white sculpture-head.

As she went rolling by Clyde's Coffee Shop, Clyde came running out. "Wait! That's my sculpture, I just loaned it to Allyson, it wasn't her's, it's mine." So Jennifer gave him the sculpture and they put it high on a shelf near the ceiling of the coffee shop.

Later Winston, Max, and I went to Clyde's shop to have a farewell cup of dark coffee. We drank the special "Allyson Blend" in memory of her. We lifted our cups and Clyde said, "Here's to you, Allyson. Good journey wherever you go."

I noticed the large sculpture-head on the deep shelf overhead. I took another rich sip of Allyson's Blend. A man inquired, "What's this about?"

Clyde served the man free coffee and answered his query, "Allyson, used to work here, she just died."

"Which one is Allyson?"

"Red-haired, fun, funny, you know, voluptuous." He made a two handed gesture to his chest.

"Oh no, not her, she was so nice. Everybody liked her. I'm so sorry. She was a good person."

I went across the street to her café' hangout. I sat down at one of Allyson's favorite tables and wrote out this notice.

Here's to announce that Allyson Bennett has died and will no longer be here to do her writing. I wanted people to know why she has disappeared. Signed, *her mom from Eugene, Oregon.*

I pinned this announcement to the bulletin board among the others: rooms to rent, "call me" notices, and advertisements of events.

Walking alone back to 949 Capp Street, I cut through the alley behind Clyde's Coffee Shop. There in the warm San Francisco sun was a sleeping bum with his back curled up against a building. I thought. *She probably talked to this man.* I looked into my purse. I'm cheap, so I hoped to find a one or a five but ironically, there was only a twenty-dollar bill. *Oh well. Here goes.* And I rolled the bill neatly and placed it into the curved hand of the sleeping man. "From Allyson," I said. Then as I walked away I thought. *Somebody will steal it from him before he wakes up.*

The apartment was empty, except for the packed suitcases bound for the airport. Everyone gathered back for the ride. Larry took the luggage to the pick-up. Uncle Lynn took the packages to be shipped to Texas. Uncle Winston swept the floor.

Rosa talked to the Chinese landlord. He yelled hysterically, "She shouldn't have died here. She should take her medicine and not have any seizures. She didn't tell me that she had epilepsy when I rented her the apartment. I didn't know that she was sick. We don't want her to die here."

Rosa negotiated for the return of the deposit and for the last month's rent, explaining, "We have cleaned the apartment. It's better than when Miss Bennett moved in."

Maybe he was worried about the ghost. Perhaps we have devalued this apartment by letting our daughter die in his place.

The landlord left. It was finished; the room was clean. We left Rosa to go through carefully to be sure that everything had been done. The family walked to the cars and the pickup truck. We stood outside the building and hugged and cried. Max did not go back to Texas. He came to Eugene with me to stay for a week.

Uncle Winston had brought his silver flute with him. He and Allyson had been flute-playing buddies. Sometimes she played with him whenever the flute was not in pawn. Today he revisited the empty apartment and played the flute. He didn't play a tune; he just let the song create itself, a sad impromptu. *Good-bye.*

We were standing on Capp St. when a telephone truck went by, waving hot wind in its wake. I was twisting and holding the piece of Allyson's hair in my hand. As the truck drove by I threw the hair into the street, letting the wind and the traffic take it away. *Was I letting go? Physically acting out letting go? But God!* There was so much more to "letting go" that I had no personal knowledge of. *World without end, Amen.*

Wednesday at 6:00 p.m. we left San Francisco. In less than three days we had disappeared Allyson's physical belongings. Her body waited in the cold at Daphne Mortuary for her ride alone to the Marin County crematorium. It would still be more than a week. In the pocket of my dramatic opera coat I put my fingers around the mini-cassette-tape from Allyson's answer machine.

Chapter Ten

Answer Machine Tape

Jazz music plays...Allyson's voice is recorded. Hi, you've reached 644-4444. Thank you for calling, please leave a message, bye. Jazz music...

#1: Hi Allyson, it's Rosie. I'm sorry I haven't got in touch with you for a while...
#2: (Man's voice.) She wore her long brown hair in a braid, rich from the smell of coffee from the café down from her house. It was Saturday evening...

#3: Hi Allyson, this is Sonja. It's nine o'clock. I'll be going to bed shortly, so call me in the morning. I should be up about 8 o'clock. Good-bye.

#4: Allyson it's Janet, we're here chanting away and wondering where you are at? Maybe you're chanting at your house. Please call back and let me know what's happening. If you need a ride and all that sort of stuff. (Sounds worried, crying?) Thank you very much.

#5: (Click, hang up.)
#6: (Click, hang up.)
#7: Hi Allyson, it's Janette. How you doing? How'd you do on the test? I felt, actually, pretty good about it. It's about 2:30 on Sunday and I'm in the mood to celebrate. It's a gorgeous sunny day. I don't know if you're up for it, but I thought since you live so close by, there's this killer pop band Brazilian samba, salsa band, playing at El Rio a place called

Your Dive. It's on Mission off of Army right next to that big Grand Auto, some kind of auto store. I don't know. They have a live band that plays out on the patio in the back and it's so cool with palm trees dancing and everyone is having such a great time. It's a real diversified crowd. If you'd like to join us there's a couple of people going, different friends I'm rounding up. I called Jackie, Kay. I called Kingman, Gary and some of his friends are coming. Hey you know the more the merrier. If you're up for it, it's 4:00 to 8:00. We're going to get there around five-ish. The band is called Tropical Breeze. If you feel like kicking up your heels and whatever and just dancing. It's a great day for it. It'll be fun. Hope to see you there. Be there. Be square. Take care.

#8: (The husky voice of Karen Red-Green.) God, I love you girl. I just called you back to hear your voice again. I'm real sorry that you didn't get to see the show at Capp Street. I'm sorry I didn't get to call you back, Friday or Saturday. And I just wanted to call you back, and hear your voice again. I love you Allyson. (Pause and very quietly.) Bye bye.

#9: Allyson, this is Karen again. I just called back to get your voice on video cassette for the tape, the *omage* that we're making, of you, to you, of your work, and works that you've been in. They will be coming to a... theatre... near... you... soon... Bye-bye, hon.

#10: (Uncle Farley's voice from Portland.)   Celeste and Winston, Ann's boyfriend Carlos Nunez, lives in Palo Alto, has a station wagon, would be happy to help with any moving problems and storage problems you have. His number is 327-3333. He's available sometime tomorrow or Wednesday to help. My thoughts are with you, and I'll be in touch with you if I can in the next couple of days.

#11: This is Lawton, (Allyson's Dad.) I'm in town. We're going out to Lynn's house. Bye. His number is 412-9999. Bye.

#12: (Allyson's ex-boyfriend.) Hi, Allyson, It's Larry. I just called to say a few things. (Big sigh.) I saw your mom today and your uncle. He seems like a really nice guy. I'm really impressed and proud of you. All your friends, your Buddhist friends, you know, told me Sunday how happy you always are. It makes me really proud. The time we were together. We both grew a lot. (Crying.) It really bothers me, that I'm so shallow, that I didn't realize it until now. (Crying.) I'm really proud of you. You are a hell of a fighter. I didn't know you were district leader until yesterday when I spoke to Kingman. That really made me proud. I'm going to bring some roses over to your house tonight...I grew 'em. Yeah, I got a garden, isn't that amazing. I actually grew some roses. I just want to say that I'm really going to miss you. I love you, Allyson. As the Buddhists might look at it—it's not good bye, it's just farewell until we meet again. So 'till next time around—*Cia,* Slim. I love you.

13: (Comic relief: The East Texas sounding voice of Max's wife.) This is Nancy. I called to see if ya'll were there yet. Mama, nobody's there; could be they're over to Uncle Lynn's house. I don't have the number there.

*   *   *

From August 1990 Allyson had been busy. She was working nine to five. In the evening she was writing a film script and helping other people with their movie projects. She had just started exercising regularly at a swimming pool. She had week-night and week-end meetings in her Buddhist groups, and practiced daily prayers called *gongyo.* In April of '91 she was studying for a Buddhist exam to raise her status. On top of all this she had a social life, and there was the mysterious male caller on her answer machine, which indicated that she had a sex life.

AJB: (From her journals.) I could start earlier if my clothes were ironed and I wasn't such a spacey woman. Time just slips through my fingers, it seems.

I need to challenge myself to get up right at 5:30 a.m. and not go for that extra 5 minutes sleep. See if an extra 5 minutes in prayer gives me more energy so I use my time better and need a little less sleep. I was encouraged yesterday at work by Diane, my boss. She said she wasn't worried about the office while she was in New York because she trusts me. I appreciate my job so much.

I just really want to chant appreciation for Larry Burnett's life. As I've been seriously striving to deepen my faith lately, I've remembered him. How young and foolish I was when I dated him and how much he put up with. I might never have started this Buddhist practice if it weren't for his patience and love. I can really see now, in retrospect how special he is and I pray for his happiness.

What is on my mind? I still keep thinking [that] something big is up-coming. Need the energy to turn it into a major victory in my life. Must create the time to chant more and more *Daimoku*.

A partner for marriage: Larry Burnett keeps coming to mind. I must chant for his happiness and appreciation for his life. I know that the best will happen. Perhaps I just need to learn appreciation for past people in my life to make the *Karma* for the right partner. Or perhaps it is Larry. I must chant patience. Feeling very impatient, want to know now who this partner will be. I can't help but feel that he (whoever this is) is in my environment and I am just waiting for the right time.

Feeling frustrated at the mess in my apartment and inability to get my work done. This is a perpetual struggle. Set goal to straighten up apartment a little each day.

Also spend a little time each week on writing my screenplay. Also really focus on [film] lighting class. Need to make most of it. Set aside more chunks of time to work on assignments.

Christmas 1990

The airplane tickets were for her holiday trip to Texas. Allyson joined the Bennett assemblage in Tyler, Texas for Christmas day dinner.

I had sent Allyson's gift to Tyler. It was a mustard-colored skirt and blouse suitable for the office work that she did. I included a fancy neck scarf. Allyson said on the phone. "Mom, it's lucky you sent me clothes, because my luggage is lost. I opened your gift early so I'd have something to wear."

A photo opportunity presented itself in the back yard by the garden gate. Here were; granddaughter Holly and her Aunt Allyson, grandpa Lawton Bennett with a bushy round gray beard and bald head, and Sarah, his dark-haired second wife. Beside them were skinny stepson Gordon, Max, looking happy to be out of Texarkana and not working, and his wife, Nancy with a strained, compulsory smile. Just as the camera snapped the picture, someone must have tickled Holly because the ten-year old was pictured swinging out to one side with an open-mouthed scream of pleasure.

Allyson wanted to be a good auntie for Holly. She had plans for the future when they could travel together.

Holly's childhood was a little different. She lived with Billie Perkins, her Texas Granny, in the back of a Victorian house and antique shop. She rode her tricycles through the dark-wood hallways among the carnival glass that tinkled as she passed. The house was musty and rambling. The old woman and the little girl shared a bed and a bedroom at the bottom of the grand staircase.

Because Nancy was mentally ill, Holly, from the time she was just two weeks old, could not stay at my son Max's home. Through the years many holiday meals had been interrupted by Nancy refusing to eat her vegetables and demanding real food,--hamburgers and Classic Coke. Nancy often became out of control with her emotions. Billie called it "showing her butt."

Allyson and I talked a lot about what should we do for Holly. I even tried to get custody of her myself, to live with me in Eugene. The best I could do was to visit every other year and during the visits to take Holly out to explore the world: To the park. And Grannie

Billie would say, "She'll fall off the swings and break her neck." To swim in Aunt Cybil's pool. "Don't take her to the pool, she'll drown." To play miniature golf. "She'll get hit by lightning."

The good thing about Holly being in Texarkana was that she had the opportunity to go to Liberty Eylau Elementary School, a school system to the South of Texarkana. Her Papa Perkins drove her there in the mornings while he was still sober, before he achieved his 12:00 o'clock drunk. Billie picked her up in the afternoons in a big air-conditioned Buick. Libery Eylau had a great music program and Holly worked with a wonderful vocal coach.

Holly had no brothers or sisters and no first cousins, not one, and no other aunts and uncles. She could ill afford the loss of her Aunt Allyson, the glamorous San Francisco woman. What would become of the years ahead, what become of their jolly travels together, what become of nighttime chats over a cup of tea. Gone were all these plans for the future that Allyson had for her niece, Holly Mae Bennett.

*   *   *

In the winter of '91 I had talked with Allyson on the phone. She told me in some detail about the movie shoots that her film group had been producing. In the big city no one owned a van or even a car; therefore, the young filmmakers had to meet on street corners by the B.A.R.T Loading themselves down with various props, lights, cameras, tri-pods, costumes, scripts, they pushed into the subway cars, and traveled to the neighborhoods of their shoots. Then, like sherpas, they exited the train and trekked, however many blocks, to apartment, street, or park for the day's movie-making assignment.

On a beautiful day in March '91, one month before her death, they took Allyson's movie shoot to a park with some drum sculptures. This is a park in San Francisco with interactive giant drums (possibly these used to be at Candlestick Park) where people are encouraged to climb up onto these drums and dance and make music. The amateur film crew made an audio tape of the sound of drums and filmed the dancers moving on the drums. At the finish they gathered to trek back to Allyson's neighborhood in the Mission District. Later, on the tape recording I was to hear a man's voice—"What kind of flowers are those?"

"Just daisies, I think." Allyson laughed. "They are daisies, aren't they?" She laughed again.

On the tape a speeding car was heard going around the corner, wheels squealing. The man's voice, with laughter, said, "Allyson, you got some sound effects there."

"Yes, I'll have to write that into the script." She laughed again.

During my months of grief I often listened to that tape recording of Allyson laughing. *Could I clone her to physically appear using the sound of her laugher?*

Part Two

Chapter Eleven

Eugene

Custom has it that when there is a death, people make a visit and bring food. This is a good idea. I was at home now, supported by a visit from my son, Max. We needed to eat. Friends came. Bonnie, from the church choir, brought peanut butter and jelly. Yvonne, from the storytelling group, brought lasagna. Michael and his daughter, from the Rose Children's Theatre, brought bakery bread.

Mary Davidson, the mother of my godsons, brought two six-packs of toilet paper. She said, "When you have a lot of company you need extra toilet paper. And besides it can be used for people who are crying."

As the visitors came into my house, I know that Barbara Snow was there, I told them, the ones that would listen, my sad story and I cried. They are brave friends that are able to walk into the home of people recently bereft. They ask themselves, "What do I say? What can I do?"

We planned a local memorial service for that week and invited our Maxwell relatives, the Bennett relatives from Portland, and friends. I hired Jon West and his wife Donna, a singing duo from Unity to provide live music. There was selected taped music.

"You're not playing 'Hey Jude' are you?" Asked my brother Winston.

"Yes," I said.

"I was afraid of that."

My son Max smoked cigarettes, so he made a ritual of sitting in the open window upstairs in my room where he enjoyed his cigarettes, blowing the smoke out into the pine tree. It looked very picturesque, him sitting there, head tilted back and knees bent.

For the memorial service, I asked this story-telling, banjo-playing son to tell the story of *Jumping Mouse,* a picture book by Hyemeyohsts Storm. The story is about a mouse who went beyond the edges of his community and traveled into the big world. The mouse had a kind and generous heart and rewarded all whom he met with gifts of his body and gifts of his spirit. At the end of the mouse's short life, eye-less, leg-less, ear-less, he transformed into an eagle.

Max wept pitifully. "I loved her so much. I can't stand the thought that she is dead. Even if she's transformed into an eagle, I don't care, I don't want her to die. Besides, I'll crackup. I won't be able to tell the story during the service without crying like an idiot."

I placed my hand on his arm. He turned away from me and looked out the window into the tree. "Max, I promise you, it will be all right. I have a friend named Christine who tells this story. I'll call her and ask her to be there as a back-up. You can begin the tale and then she'll step in if needed. I really want you to participate."

Later Uncle Winston agreed to accompany the story with some Native American riffs on his flute.

I have a beautiful bed with a 1970s velvet patchwork quilt in jewel colors: gold, purple, ruby, amber. One afternoon before the memorial service, I was resting on the bed and I remembered that I wanted to tell Christine about the story of *Jumping Mouse,* so I rolled to my left side and reached for the telephone. "Hello, Christine, this is Celeste."

Christine was horrified. She knew of my tragedy. Even before I asked the favor she said, "Oh no, Celeste, no!"

I gasped, saliva bubbling between my lips. "Christine, I have a favor to ask."

Christine repeated, "No, oh no. I'm so sorry, oh Celeste."

My voice was choking with tears and I asked her the favor. "At the memorial service for my daughter, my son Max is telling the story of *Jumping Mouse.* In case he becomes too emotional to continue, maybe you could step in to help him finish. My daughter, Allyson, went to London, she saw *Cats,* she toured the Scottish castles. In San Francisco she always stopped to hang out with the street people, the poor, the crazies. She shared what little she had.

The story of *Jumping Mouse* is a good metaphor for her life. And kind of Buddhist too."

"Yes, of course, I will be there, but I'm sure that your son will do fine. Anyway, if he needs me I will be there. Good-bye, sweetie, you get some rest."

"Thank you, Christine." Still barely audible, my voice was covered in sobbing.

*   *   *

My brother Farley Maxwell, a United Church of Christ preacher, brought a cassette tape of the song Memories by Andrew Lloyd Webber from *Cats*. In his talk he remembered that Allyson, our little mouse, went to London and saw the musical *Cats*. It was a three-handkerchief song. "Touch me, it's so easy to leave me, all alone with the memory…"

Because of her being Buddhist, we wanted a neutral space for the memorial service so we planned it to take place in my friend Jerry Williams's house. Jerry's living room had an open area with four white columns rising to a skylight. In this shaft of sunlight, or Oregon gloom, there were trees and plants and hanging bird cages with singing canaries. Interestingly enough, for decorative purposes only, he had a few Buddhist statues, along with several goddess idols and a Ganesha, the elephant god of India.

Jerry prepared the way from the freeway I – 5 to exit #91, by marking the way to his house with purple balloons. (Funny, Allyson exited in '91.) The memorial was attended by a small group of people, mostly my friends. Allyson's friends were married or working and living in widely diverse towns, states, and countries. I believe that Coco's mother was there, but then we hadn't prepared a guest book, so I had no way of knowing who came.

Brother Farley and his wife Mary, their son Julio, Brother Winston and his wife Llew, attended, of course, and so did Allyson's Aunt Sally, Winston's first wife. My ex-husband's family came from Portland, Allyson's Uncle Jim and Aunt Lee and maybe some of the Bennett cousins.

My agreement with myself, as before, was that I would allow myself to act authentically, which meant that I would surely cry. And I allowed, of course, other people to cry. It was not to be a Presbyterian service. We took turns speaking. Max successfully told the story of *Jumping Mouse,* accompanied by Uncle Winston's flute. Christine was massively relieved that she didn't have to jump in to finish the tale. The musicians from Unity Church, sang a song about dancing shoes, "Grace" by Melissa Javors, 1982. "The proof of God's grace in this crazy ol' place is that anyone dances at all."

We finished with the Beatles and "Hey, Jude" with all of us swaying and crying. "Remember to let her into your heart, and you can start to make it better. Da Da Da ..." There is a place on the tape where the Beatles scream "Judy, Judy, Judy!" Some of us let go and screamed. Probably that was I. Others did not choose to participate in the screaming.

I know intellectually that it was right for me to scream at my child's funeral. But I worried then and still worry about what other people thought. Particularly, I felt ashamed in front of my ex-husband's brother from Portland and his family to see me screaming and acting dramatic. I felt self-conscious for my ex-sister-in-law Sally Maxwell to see me this way, stripped of any social graces at all. I worried about her sitting on the floor, (she did not have a chair,) whereas Llew sat in a chair next to Winston.

When the people left, I was alone with Jerry. I must have said something against Max. I don't know what. Anyway, Jerry came to me. Jerry knows a lot about family strife--he is gay and his large family is Reform Mormons. He was the only son along with his mother's four daughters, and Jerry was a twin with his sister, Judy. I was sitting in an ornate Bankokian armchair and he came and leaned over me, placing a hand on each side. He said, "Listen to me, Missy, yes, you are grieving the death of your daughter, but you have to remember that you have a wonderful son and he is very much alive. Whatever is wrong between you and him, you must fix it and you need to cherish him."

Dear Celeste,

I'm sitting here listening to the tape you sent me. It's beautiful! I especially like the song "Dancing Shoes", it's so Allyson. It sings of her gentle beauty. She always loved to dance.

As I sit here and listened I'm so sad. I haven't seen Allyson for over a year. I thought about her a lot but was always too busy to call. I'm so mad at myself for this! I never thought it would be any big deal, it was the way our friendship was…no matter how long we were apart, I knew I could call and she would be there for me (and I for her)…but she's not here anymore. I can't believe it…

I really wanted to see her. I've been doing a lot of growing spiritually lately and she is the only person I know that truly knows me that I can talk to about this stuff without feeling like a pest.

She was such a good friend. This accepting side of Allyson I see in you. I want you to know that she thought the world of you and the rest of the family. Remember when she and I had "my first Thanksgiving turkey? We didn't put the turkey into the oven until 2:00 p.m.

Anyways – when we finally sat down , many hours later, we decided we should talk about what we were thankful for. Our first toast was to our families. I know if Allyson could tell you anything it would be that she couldn't have had a better mother.

With all the love you have for Allyson I know you are probably hurting deeply inside. I wish I could do something to stop the pain. That's the hardest thing about death, the pain of those left behind.

My pain is eased somewhat by my belief that Allyson's death meant that she had completed her lessons in this life and she is moving onto an even greater understanding and peaceful life.

When my father died I explained it as, "He earned his right to die." At the time I didn't look at it quite the way I do now. But it seemed the only justification for why such a good person would die. Now I understand that we don't really die, we just move on...From a mouse into an eagle. I feel proud for Allyson that she made it.

I will be coming up to Eugene the second week in July. I would be honored to go with you to sprinkle her ashes – it would mean a lot to me.

Hang in – I love you! -
See you soon Coco.

*   *   *

After all of the funereal songs and dances ended, the mess cleared away and the friends and relations departed on airplanes, trains, cars and buses, I stood in the middle of my living room, my heart totally broken. I spoke out loud, "What do I do now?"

A low, booming voice, perhaps James Earl Jones, came inside my mind, "Call Sacred Heart Hospital."

I called.   That is when I found the Bereavement Support Group that is provided by Hospice of Sacred Heart. This group meets once a week on Wednesdays from 4:00 to 6:00 p.m. I am a dramatic person and I do well in groups, so for the next two years I began to mark my days from Wednesday to Wednesday.   The first year I attended once a week; the second year I went every other week. I called it *Grief Class*. The rest of the time I did my puppeteering and theatre work, combed through Allyson's papers and bills, and even filed her taxes! (Yes, dead people have to file their taxes.) I always looked forward to Wednesday afternoons.   Like Scarlet O'Hara, I could "Think about that tomorrow."

Dorothy was a friend from Junior High and beyond. She lived near Houston, Texas. In the next few years she was to suffer from the loss of her wonderful husband through cancer, but she did not like group therapy.   Her style of grief was to crawl into the dark closet, hold on to his slippers, and whimper to herself. From time to time she was rescued by a neighbor, an RN, who came to pound on her door until Dorothy showed herself. The neighbor woman would then drag the newly-made widow outside for exercise, fellowship and sun. But solitude in a dark closet was not my style. I needed to be with other people who shared similar sorrows.

My first day at the Sacred Heart Bereavement Group, I walked into the counseling center and asked directions. I walked ten steps down the hall, slumped against the wall, and broke totally into gasping sobs. The receptionist pressed a button marked "grieving person collapsed in the hallway" and one of the counseling staff came to lead me to the end of the long corridor. A volunteer made me a nametag, patted me on the head, and gave to me my own personal large box of Kleenex.

After that, I had a personal joke. I could always spot the new people because they were crying uncontrollably. Others among us were relaxed and happy, smiling and talking, waiting for the meeting to begin. Joining the circle, our leader, Marcia Hilton, would say, "I see that we have a few new people, with us today." Looking around the room, I could pick out the new people whose faces were buried in tissues from their own personal large-sized box of Kleenex.

By the time of her memorial celebration, I had already reasoned that it was OK for Allyson to die early. It was her business. But it was not OK for me to lose such an important person. At the Bereavement Group, the sayings are: *When your parents die you lose your past. When your spouse dies, you lose your present. When your children die, you lose your future.*

Chapter Twelve

Mother's Day

Three weeks after Allyson's death it was Mother's Day. I did not go to the Unity Church that day. I had attended services for two Sundays, where I hugged and was hugged. I felt a strong need to let the church know my story that I was suffering from the death of my daughter. The community acknowledged what had happened, but I found it embarrassing to have people look at me. I could not pray or sing or *listen*. I was self-absorbed.

My friend and fellow puppeteer Deb Chase came from Portland to be with me. We hiked up Mt. Pisgah on a steep meadow trail. The wild irises were blooming. I had to move slowly because of being out of shape, but also I was just so tired from grieving. My spirit and body were heavy. We walked to the top and found a place in the clearing. Sitting on top of the hill, looking down at the North Fork of the Willamette River, I put my head on Deb's lap as she stroked my hair.

*   *   *

Daily I received a lot of cards and letters of condolence. I told our letter carrier about the death in the family. One day in May, the ashes arrived by U.S. Mail from the Daphne Funeral Home. Through the closed curtain I saw the shadow of the mail carrier pass the living room window. He knocked. I opened the door, looking like a housewife in my butcher's-cut apron.

He said, "I brought you your daughter."

It was a brown-paper-wrapped parcel the size of a shoebox. With two hands I took it from him. It was heavy, maybe ten pounds, as if it was loaded with sand.

I said, "Oh, that's really strange."

"Yes, it is strange to deliver remains through the mail."

"Have you ever done this before?"

"No, this is the first time."

"Oh my," I said. He stepped back and I stepped back. Turning away from the daylight, I walked back into the dark of my cave house. I sat down in the big chair by the curtained window. No work would get done that day. I sat and held the baby-sized package in the crook of my arm, rocking in the chair. Then I put them to rest, that's what I did. For several months, I did not open the cremains while they rested in a hidden nook of my sewing closet.

*   *   *

Mother came to my house and brought a nice little dogwood tree in a can. It was *Cornus florida*, a pink dogwood, a tree to remember Allyson by. Yvonne Young brought a Peace Rose, also in a can. These things sat in the sun and the rain on the patio behind my house. My housemate Suzette watered the plants to keep them alive. I wanted to kick them, I hated these wonderful gifts. I wanted to stamp them to pieces. *Anger.*

"I don't want any god-damned plants to put in my yard. I don't want a stupid tree to remember her by. I want my daughter back!"

Somehow it was decided where to put the plants and Suzette very kindly and gently planted these offerings and tended them throughout the heat of summer, the tree to the right of the front door and the rose on the back east corner of the house where the morning sun would dry the leaves, protecting it from rose blight.

*   *   *

Mary and Dale Davidson and my nine-and six-year-old godsons Brad and Teddy invited me to their house. I answered, "I don't feel well, but I'd love to come anyway."

"You don't have to do anything. Just be here with us and we'll go on about our business. I just thought you might want to be with people a little bit."

"Thank you, Mary, that will be great."

I went to their house in east Springfield and laid on the couch in the family room. They worked and played and went in and out all afternoon and evening. Every once in a while Mary would stop and pat me. I heard Mary telling Teddy, "She's so sad because her daughter has died and she will be sad for a very long time. If anything ever happened to you or Brandon, I would be sad forever and ever."

The boys hardly talked to me, but just having them near was a comfort.

*   *   *

In this stage of my grief, my body felt like someone had filled my veins with molten lead. To climb the stairs to my studio was a heavy trip: my shoulders stooped, my head weighted down, each leg an immoveable object. Going up the sixteen steps, I had to pull myself up by the handrail, as if to climb a mountain.

But I had to create the summer show for the state libraries. I had to build the props, and create the marionettes. I worked slowly. The art work I did was heavy looking and the proportions were strange. The heads were small and the bodies wide and heavy, reminding me of the work of Modigliani. Sometimes I sat in the chair by the window and could not move or work at all. Just sitting for many hours.

I received a phone call from Allyson's insurance from the American Association for the Blind. There was a death benefit. $10,000. I spoke to the person on the phone, said thank you, and hung up. From the window ledge and the lotus flower picture, I received a message from Allyson, "All right Mom!" Followed by a thumbs up sign.

I let out a blood-curdling scream and collapsed. At the other end of the house, David Stelle, one of my housemates, heard the scream. He had become used to my expressions of grief, but this one was different. He crept slowly to the bottom of the stairs. He listened and heard choking and bumping sounds. He spoke my name and came on up. I was in the middle of the floor pulled into a ball, pitifully sobbing. My legs were pumping in a running motion. I was bumping and thrashing with my left shoulder and head arched downward. I was grinding my head and face into the floor.

I moaned, "They're giving me money."

To be rewarded for such a loss was just horrible. It was blood money. I could not swallow this news, It felt like I could not breathe.

David, the brave soul, waded through the charged air in the room and came onto the floor with me. He grabbed for my head trying to protect me from the bumping. My emotional reaction was eerily similar to an epilepsy seizure. He hauled my top end onto his lap.

I tried to tell him what had happened. He didn't try to stop my reaction, he just was physically and comfortingly there. When the spasm past, I sat still for the rest of the week, waiting for Wednesday afternoon to come, so that I could go to my Grief Group.

*   *   *

By mid June the preparations for the marionette show "Red Riding Hood and Hunker Jaw the Wolf," were finished. I rehearsed and loaded the Maxima station wagon for the summer tour. I drove from Eugene to Reedsport, then down Highway #101 to the Coos Bay Public Library, one hundred miles from Eugene. There I performed two shows. I was funny, energetic, and I worked the marionettes with the skill of many years' experience. Afterwards, I felt like the movie-boxer, Rocky had smashed me onto the ropes of the ring. I was punchy. I couldn't put together a sentence. I was exhausted and on the verge of tears. Using the new ramp and wheeled puppet box, I loaded up the show into the back of the Maxima and drove down to the cliffs near Shore Acres Park. I did not hike or walk on the beach because I was too exhausted. I opened up the car windows and the sun roof and let the ocean breezes in, though near Coos Bay, the wind is more like a blast than a breeze. I cried, slept, and read a book without leaving the car for four hours. The book was a paperback, *Blossom,* a story of a woman investigating her sister's death. It was scary and gruesome and just the kind of book that I could relate to.

*   *   *

I found a little heart-shaped black-gold ring amongst Allyson's jewelry. It became a memory ring for me to wear on my pinkie. Touching the ring throughout the days of my mourning gave me some comfort. This day, overlooking the Pacific Ocean, I noticed that the garnet had fallen out of the ring. (Allyson's birthday was January 3. Mine is January 23. The birthstone for January is garnet.) After I drove back into Coos Bay and ate clam chowder at Mo's restaurant, I stopped at the jeweler in the rustic shopping mall. I cried, of course, as I explained to the clerk that I needed a replacement stone for this ring. I said, "I'll be back here in a couple of weeks. If it's all right, I can pick up the ring then."

Another day I took the puppet show to Corvallis. Afterwards, driving on the highway, I began to cry again. I was alone in the car on a busy road and thought that I could scream and no one would hear me. So I yelled out and made noise. My jaw began to vibrate and I made noises like the broken transmission of my old van. My eyes streamed with tears and then I couldn't see the road. I had to find a place to pull over before I wound up in an accident. There on the edge of the road I continued to cry for twenty minutes or so. I wept with such intensity that it caused physical pain in the solar plexus: actual heartache.

I reported to the Bereavement Support Group, "I am so tired of crying. I feel as though the weeping will go on forever."

Another time I broke down in tears at the Taco Time restaurant during lunch. There among the cheerful hubbub of activity, across from people standing in line waiting to order, I sat and cried into my tostada. Other customers sat around the faux adobe room, leaning forward and eating tacos that fall apart at the first bite. Children swung their legs and fat people slid their big tummies behind the tables, smacking their lips in anticipation. In the corner of the room here I was, a chubby, older woman with pewter-colored hair, my nose and eyes red from crying, eating my noon meal with tears dripping down. I stopped eating to wipe my eyes and blow my nose, then I ate some more. Life goes on. I have to keep eating and I have to keep crying. *How many days and hours is enough? How many buckets full?*

People stared at me, or they purposely did *not* stare at me. Being a crying woman is like having only one leg. People look or avert their eyes. No one ever asked me, "Why are you crying?" Is that a rude question? Like asking, "What happened to your leg?"

I love kids because they're so direct. "Wow, where's your leg?"

"It got wounded and the doctor cut it off. They threw it in a bucket."

"Gees, that's awful!"

"Yeah, it's awful, but you get used to it."

Well, what happened to me was awful and I was *not* going to get used to it. Here I was moving around the world with a broken heart with no way to hide because of my tears. That was funny. I said, what was "happening" to me? But nothing "happened" to me. What happened, happened to Allyson. She was the one who died. All that happened to me was that I got left behind. Time heals all wounds, they say, and like a prisoner I had to put in my time. Doing my time. One day at a time. Keeping my nose clean.

*   *   *

In Mexico there is a story of a woman, La Llorona, who married a handsome and successful ranchero. They had two children, a little girl and a little boy, but after a while her husband left her, coming home only to pay attention to the two children. La Llorona became jealous of her children and impetuously drowned them in the river. La Llorona immediately regretted what she had done and tried to save them, but there was nothing she could do, her children were dead, so this dark-eyed, dark-haired woman followed them into the black waters and into her own death.

Supposedly a true story, the tale is often repeated of the ghost of La Llorona who walks the streets of the little Mexican town and along the shores of the river calling for her children. "*Mis hijos, mis hijos!* ¿Dónde están mis hijos? *Mis Hijos, mis hijos.* Where are my children?" She moans and cries, her hair long and scraggly, her teeth black and rotten. "*Mis hijos, mis hijos.*"

*   *   *

I lost my daughter. Therefore I lost one of my hobbies, daughter-watching. "What is your daughter doing lately?" I answered that she is making movies, got a new apartment, has a new boyfriend, etc. *Is that all she was? A topic of conversation? A preoccupation of my mind? An identity? I have a daughter; therefore, I am.*

What do I do now with Allyson's beautiful dollhouse? My granddaughter doesn't want it. Holly's other grandmother left her plenty of antiques.

I missed the identity of being a Mom. I might as well have never married and never had children. My son is far away and has his own life. He's a boy, and never writes, never calls. He cares for me in the broad sense of *I have a mom in Oregon who is really great.* I sound like a Jewish mama: "He doesn't feel it necessary to contact me on a weekly basis or even on a monthly basis. He thinks that once or twice a year is sufficient. Sufficient for whom? Not me. *Oy Vey.*"

I guess, most of all, or should I say, worst of all, is that I lost my contact with God/Goddess/ Higher Power. My spiritual life had been, until then, consistent all my life. I've always had an ongoing relationship with God. I must confess it's been a fairly light weight relationship, an easy-way-out-religion, nothing profound. For some years I had developed a morning meditation that was comforting and invigorating. I went to church on Sundays and enjoyed the people, the singing, and some of the preaching. I am more than a bit of a feminist and have been consistently prickly about all the God-equals-male-person-He-stuff. Allyson had complained to me that she had the same trouble with the patriarchy of Buddhism. I welcomed the Presbyterian's well-intentioned attempts at inclusive language, like Creator or Parent, or the AA concept of Higher Power.

God was with me 100% of the time at Allyson's death and during the two or three weeks that followed. But God left me as thoroughly as Allyson. I turned around and found to my surprise that Higher Power had left me alone. Totally cut off, I could not dance and I could not pray. My prayers took the form of a child's tantrum, like the fits I threw when my Dad left for war. "I want my daughter back! I want my daughter back! I do not want to live! I want my daughter back!"

This is one of the seven deadly steps of grief. *Anger*. I had been an angry five-year-old about my Dad's death those past forty-plus years ago. Anger can be a very long step. *Is this why I have always been fat? Am I eating to stuff down anger?*

Chapter Thirteen

Dreams

Rosa called. She had two dreams about Allyson. I had not had any dreams since the ice lake vision. I was feeling lonely and cut off from contact with my dead daughter. *Why doesn't she call, why doesn't she write? Grown children are so inconsiderate of their parents.*

Both Rosa's dreams had to do with the empty apartment. Rosa, no doubt, had been traumatized by being the last one in Allyson's apartment.

Dream number one: The afternoon light came through the bay windows, shining on the wood floors, the room echoing with emptiness. In the closet was Allyson's skin hanging on a hook. Then Allyson came swooping back into her skin and danced around her empty rooms.

Rosa's other dream: There is the empty room with the sunlight shining through the windows. A box of baby things sits in the middle of the room with a few toys   scattered here and there. A large tree breaks up through the middle of the wood floor, it is like an oak tree without leaves, pushing up boards with its sturdy tree trunk with reaching limbs. The tree grows into the room, filling the space and more limbs break out through the window-glass reaching toward the world outside.

My thoughts, from what Rosa said to me over the phone that night, were of the strength and power of the tree; of the sexual thrust through the floor; of a presence being made known; the baby toys, a rebirth.

Chapter Fourteen

London

In January 1983, Allyson took Peter Egan's theatre class at Mills College, in which the students traveled to London to attend shows for several weeks. He often worked as a visiting lecturer at Mills. She went to London as a little Oregon mouse in the big city.

The college students were all invited to the Egan's London house for tea. The young ladies, dressed in the finest clothes that they could pull from their travel bags, took public transportation out to the Egan's suburban home.

Tea was served and everyone sat in a gracious circle, straight-backed, ankles crossed, little fingers bent, enjoying tea and sandwiches with these generous and loving Londoners. The rattle of delicate china cups and saucers filled the silences between gay, mostly theatre, topics of conversation.

AJB: I loved the Egan's cats – especially after seeing *Cats* the night before. I had a whole new perspective. One cat was absolutely gorgeous, an Abyssinian, and it looked exacted like their daughter Rebecca. Then there was a huge, fuzzy gray cat that was really stupid. He gets turned on by 100% wool, and proceeded to lick the wall and stare amorously at my cashmere sweater. The third cat was all black, and was named Macavity as a kitten because of his personality, but alas his personality underwent a major transformation when he was fixed, so they now call him Mac.

*   *   *

The young visitors, two by two, took their leave and suddenly Allyson Bennett from Eugene, Oregon, found that she was the last guest and didn't know how to say good-bye. (I mentioned before that she was at heart a shy creature and had only recently learned how to fake self-confidence.) So she sat there like a stump gathering moss. The Egan's went from tea to sherry, talking between themselves, and Allyson had a few drinks and kept sitting there in the lovely English drawing room. The rain fell outside and the January dark flowed over the suburban streets. Soon they asked her to supper and she didn't know how to say no or good-bye so she joined them and after a very long visit, Peter organized a ride for her and sent her back to her hotel.

This tea party in London was contrasted by another night at Covent Gardens during a riotous evening in which some of her fellow students met some English punks. The year, as I said was 1983. The Mills students sat in a roaring pub and flirted and talked to boys with spiked hair, chains, and piercings. Here Allyson had one of the many opportunities--that she didn't take--to lose her firmly ensconced virginity.

AJB: The first thing that hit me about being back in California was being surrounded by all these harsh American accents. They sounded almost as odd as English accents had when I first arrived in London.

The second thing that hit me – climate shock. It was warm! Like short sleeve weather. And the sun was out – I at least expected rain.

Chapter Fifteen

All Alone

This is about death, better stop here. *Not me, not mine.* When
Allyson died, my cry went up, "Why?" Shakespeare speaks it for me:
<u>King John. Act III Scene iv,</u>
King Phillip: Patience, good lady! Comfort, gentle Constance!
Constance: No, I defy all counsel, all redress.
Death, death; O amiable lovely death!
Thou odoriferous stench! Sound rottenness!
Arise forth from the couch of lasting night,
Thou hate and terror to prosperity,
And I will kiss thy detestable bones
And put my eyeballs in thy vaulty brows
And ring these fingers with thy household worms
And stop this gap of breath with fulsome dust
And be a carrion monster like thyself:
Come, grin on me, and I will think thou smilest
And buss thee as thy wife. Misery's love,
O come to me!...

I will not having breath to cry:
O, that my tongue were in the thunder's mouth!
Then with a passion would I shake the world;
And rouse from sleep that fell anatomy
Which cannot hear a lady's feeble voice,
Which scorns a modern invocation....

I am not mad; this hair I tear is mine;
My name is Constance; I was Geffrey's wife;
Young Arthur is my son, and he is lost;

I am not mad: I would to heaven I were!
For then, 'tis like I should forget myself:
O, if I could, what grief should I forget!...
If I were mad; too well, too well I feel
The different plague of each calamity...
I shall not know him: therefore never, never
Must I behold my pretty Arthur more.

Grief fills the room up of my absent child,
Lies in his bed, walks up and down with me,
Puts on his pretty looks, repeats his words,
Remembers me of all his gracious parts,
Stuffs out his vacant garments with his form;
Then, have I reason to be fond of grief?...

O Lord! My boy, my Arthur, my fair son!
My life, my joy, my food, my all the world!
My widow-comfort, and my sorrows' care!

Processing this event went on for several years, and who says that it has stopped as of this writing? "Why?" Well, there's death and taxes. What else is sure? Birth is. At the present state of medical science, birth still involves a working womb. For the body, what else is sure? I suppose gravity. We mostly can rely on the leaping human to eventually return to earth. Even our darling astronauts must put an end to floating in space. I'll say "gravity" is sure because for the first year of my learning to live without my daughter I spent most of my time falling to the floor in great travail or trying to lift my heavy head out of agony.

Question. How come a healthy twenty-seven-year-old dies suddenly when my mother, an ancient, gasping old woman, keeps on ticking? To quote Charlie Brown, "Aargh!"

Sister-in-law Mary Maxwell said, "Celeste, she had epilepsy!"

But that's no answer. People with epilepsy don't necessarily die young. They control their condition with life-style changes and medications. Therefore, this grieving matron sits down to figure it out on paper.

In my immediate family, twenty-two people have died in the last 100 years.

1. Two infants during birth, 1905 – 1912.

2. Two twenty-something mothers during labor, 1905 – 1912.

3. Forty-year-old grandfather and his four-year-old son die in a 1912 auto accident at the speed of 25 miles an hour, no other cars involved. Death by mishap.

4. Sixty-five-year-old lovable drunken maternal grandfather died of alcoholism, 1938.

5. One-armed Civil War veteran died in his dotage, after finishing his memoirs, 1930s.

6. Here we are, these buried children, my stepfather's only child: My twenty-seven-year-old distraught stepbrother commits suicide with a rifle, first, taking his wife Linda and two-year-old daughter, Denise, with him. Murder-suicide. That's grim. Somehow adding to this tragedy was the fact that Linda was German and Denise was German and adopted. 1964.

7. Forty-year-old brothers, my father and my uncle: one died in a Japanese prison camp, the other of leukemia. 1945.

8. Step-grandmother Hilda Parmenter died of cancer, 1929.

9.Lastly, the Grim Reaper harvests his aged ones:
      Grandmother at one-hundred-and-one, 1982.
      Step-father eighty-eight, 1998.
       Mother at ninety-nine, 2008.
      Aunt Louise, Uncle Frank, and elderly cousins, Dorothy,
          Jim and Joe 1998 – 2008.

<u>Total died in our family: 22</u>
4 below age of five
4 young adults
4 forty-year-olds
1 sixty-year-old
9 over the age of eighty.

Everybody else in the family is hanging-in with anticipations of the great sights and sounds ahead in the year 2000 and beyond. I did not mention my twenty-seven-year-old daughter. She cannot be added to this historical list among the dead. She does not belong yet, not just yet.

One of Allyson's Buddhist teachers felt that she had reentered quickly into her next life. *Should I go looking for a child who is Allyson and have her again in my life?* That is a comforting thought but an impossible task. She died because she was needed in a next life for a purpose? It is reassuring to those left behind, to feel that our loved ones died for a "porpoise."

For me I felt angry towards my dog, a pomi-poo, of all people. My dog's name was Jessie and she was not a really young dog and not particularly the most exciting dog I ever had in my life. I looked at my dog and said, "Why aren't you dead? Why didn't you die instead of Allyson?" They call this, I believe, "bargaining." *What is this dog still doing here?*

My stepfather was ornery and had been sick for years, a true pain in the ass, which incidentally was where his own pain was located, in the lower lumbar area. I felt that he was no earthly good to anyone and yet he remained living while my most valuable daughter was dead. *How can you figure? What are the rules for who dies?*

At this time, April 1991, thousands of little Bangladesh children were dying of starvation. At the heavenly gates did Allyson have to wait in line with these children to be processed or was she pushed ahead because she was a college graduate? Jim Henson, the creator of Sesame Street puppets, died May 1990 at age 53. I hoped that he was still hanging around in the orientation area waiting for young adult children of puppeteers to be greeted. I imagined Allyson running up to him. "My mother is a puppeteer living in Eugene, Oregon. She performs mainly with marionettes."

"Hello, Allyson," answers the gracious Mr. Henson. "Welcome to paradise. I believe I remember her from the puppeteer convention in Nashville. Chubby, thin hair, red nose? A bit of a Cookie Monster herself. Ha ha." He pats his white-robe-clad tummy.

Allyson laughs her short staccato laugh, "That sounds like her."

I thought, *what if she stayed at home with me after she became an adult and I could have protected her from her seizures? Shouldn't we have a category of what ifs as part of the seven steps of grieving. What ifs and If onlys and why, why, whys?*

The Unity preacher, Bill Wilson, came to call. He said, "If she had chosen to live with you, she would have waited until you went to the grocery store and then she would have jumped upside down in the bathtub and died anyway."

When you gotta go, you gotta go.

Death is very much, truly, like the figure cloaked in a hoodie and carrying a scythe. Enter the Grim Reaper. *Swish* goes the cutting tool. Down fall the creatures that are in the path of destruction. What if you bend over to smell the flowers? Then you escape because the blade passes over your head. Toddlers who leap for joy and get in the way of the swinging scythe, must die, down they go, soon to sprout wings, joining the ranks of chubby cherubs. Old, feeble people shrink with age. That's why a lot of elders stay alive so long, they're short, they bend over to cough, they fall asleep in the harvest field, the scythe passes a foot above their heads.

Early on, I came to the conclusion that Allyson's death was not the tragic death of a woman with a brilliant future. I knew deep in my heart that her death was her own. Why? She died because she had come to the end of her short life. For whatever reason, she had died early. It's just like grown kids to go and do what they have to do without consulting their parents. "Mom, I'm moving to Australia for the next 20 years. I'll keep in touch." Or in the old days when grown children moved across America in covered wagons and parents never heard from them again…ever. Were they dead? Et by a bear? Or were they somewhere in the west having a wonderful life.

Like climbing baby spiders, fresh from their eggs, they move up to the tallest part of the tree. Remember Charlotte's little darlings? They walk to the end of the limb and, when the spring breezes blow, each lets out a single silver thread from one of their spinnerets, which carries them away. In the spider world this is called parachuting.

In the old days when couples had a dozen children, some stayed home and others moved on. Now, with the smaller families, we expect our children to stay in touch forever. I even heard once that there used to be a custom where one child, usually a daughter, was designated to never marry and to work forever as a servant for her parents. Cinderella was r-e-a-l. No wonder Lizzie Borden took an ax.

People said to me, " It is so difficult to lose a child." But Allyson was not a child, she was my adult, and not only was she my adult child, but also she was a friend. We had achieved, I thought, the honored state of adult-to-adult relationship.

*   *   *

In 1941 I was almost three years old when my soldier Daddy went to war. Because he had been my number one, my baby life crashed around me. Mother supervised the packing of all of our belongings into a moving van and took my two older brothers, the maid, and me on a long train ride from Fort Douglas, Utah, to a little town called Columbus, Kansas, with the dog Judy howling unhappily in a crate with the luggage. All the way to our new home, I similarly howled. "I want my Daddy! I want my Daddy!"

For the long years of the war, Daddy was a prisoner of the Japanese, mostly at Camp Cabanatuan in the Philippines. I prayed daily, kneeling with my little chubby knees, on the carpeted stairs to our upstairs apartment. " Oh God, please bring my Daddy home to me." After holding on for four years, Daddy died in 1945 during the liberation, drowned during transport on a Japanese prison ship. I remember the arrival of the notification telegram. It was Christmas time and we were all at Grandmother's farm in Tuscaloosa, Alabama. I was sick that day and was in Grandma's big bed. Mother and Grandmother (Daddy's mother) stood side by side, with the telegram between them. Neither wanted to open it. I don't know if they told me that Daddy had died, or if they read it out loud, or if I just knew in my little-girl heart what was going on. I stood on the bed and jumped up and down, my Shirley Temple curls bouncing around my head, and I screamed again, over and over… "I want my Daddy! I want my Daddy!"

In the 1940s little children did not go to counselors. We were not allowed to feel bad. My mother, however, went through the grieving widow phase; she received lots of support for her suffering. She was even famous, a genuine war widow! I believe that we children were distracted from our suffering. People took us on pony rides or gave us presents. "Here, child, have a cookie." People did not want to see the children crying. So what became of our grief? I remember seeing the movie, *Lassie Come Home.* I reacted with floods of tears to that movie. I cried about that movie for at least six months. Mother or the maid would say, "Celeste, honey, what is wrong?"

I answered, "Lassie come home. Lassie come home."

"It's all right child. Here, have a cookie." The cookie became what is known as a *secondary gain,* which is a reward for travail. The counselor might ask, "What is the payoff for the suffering you have endured?"

What was my secondary gain?

Like the dirty old man who gave me soda pop in exchange for feeling me up.

Like being overweight, which kept me from having to deal with the   dating world.

Like getting special love and attention when I cried for the death of my daughter.

There had been other deaths of friends and family over the years, but these were special: the two deaths of my most important people, my Daddy and my adult child Allyson.

Chapter Sixteen

August, 1990

In San Francisco, Allyson finally found a career placement position, working for a woman named Diane with the American Association for the Blind.   Allyson organized meetings and conferences, booked hotels and conference rooms, reserved banquet halls, called in orders for hundreds of box lunches. She coordinated participants' arrivals and departures from the airports and trains and supplied transportation to the hotels and conference sites. For the visually impaired clients she provided one-on-one assistants to help them negotiate the big city.

She felt that her new employers accepted her seizure disorder partly because the organization served a special population. At that time she had been seizure-free for all of 1990. At her Buddhist altar, she had chanted for healing. She also used acupuncture, and was following a daily health plan of diet and exercise. Then in March of 1991, she got up from her office desk and went into the hall and was hit with a seizure, which pulled her violently forward, and slammed her backward into a door jam. She fell to the floor, eye- balls rolled back, and lay there going through the gentle tremors that marked the ending of the episode. An ambulance was called, and she had to face the cost of a trip to the ER. After this, her shoulder bothered her so she had been going to the doctor and to physical therapy for the last three weeks. After her death on April 21, I used her calendar and her address book to call the doctor and the physical therapist to cancel all her future appointments. "Allyson has died." I told them.

Her boss Diane was upset and sorry. She had been totally happy with Allyson as her assistant. The office delivered flowers to the apartment with a box of Allyson's personal belongings. There was no briefcase containing the film script that she had been writing and later Diane reported that no script was found in the desk or on the office computer.

*   *   *

During college she managed the bills through a generous scholarship from Mills and monthly payments from her dad, Lawton Bennett. Lawton helped send Allyson through school, and he also sent me through the Drama Department at the University of Oregon. He paid for his second wife, Sarah, in her studies. He had a Ph.D. in Political Science and he was a promoter of higher education for others.

Mills College's scholarship committee was interested in single mothers, working mothers, and particularly artists; therefore, through my low-income, self-employed puppet theatre I also helped to qualify her for this educational experience. Every year in January, I had to hurry to file my income tax and get the numbers to the college.

The Mills College campus is in Oakland and is surrounded by some unsafe neighborhoods. Early on, when Allyson visited the campus, traveling alone, we would have mother-daughter workshops about personal safety.

1. When walking on the street, keep a proud, confident posture with a no- nonsense, don't-tread-on-me attitude.

2. When possible, carry a heavy umbrella as a weapon.

3.After late-night study or work sessions wait for a ride from the Mills security van that loops the campus every twenty minutes.

*   *   *

AJB: [About Larry Burnett.] We met the last weekend in February at the Café Picaro. It was the end of the *Sakabuku* campaign. [*Sakabuku* means to set a goal and to move toward that to success.*]* My Buddhist friend Will was set on a *Shakabuku*, you were set on getting laid. I was set on being depressed about Paul, my

Christmas fling, to whom I was in the process of writing yet another tearful letter of love to be posted to Boston. You didn't get laid that weekend, but I did figure out I liked you and I left the door open for possibilities. I just had to figure out my feelings. There was still this far away vision of Paul, my great love, on the other coast. But you were here. And you were relatively patient and sweet. Although "maybe" to you meant yes, with some sweet and sweaty persuasion. A week passed, and our first date was delayed as you stood me up and I was ill. But I am forgiving and invited you out to tea at the Japanese Tea Gardens.

I warned you not to touch me. "You'll contract this nasty cold." I said. But you didn't care. You finally broke through my maybes.

I remember specifically how I felt after we first made love. I was lying on top of you with my head next to yours, face down in the pillow crying. I gained some measure of control and said, "You aren't planning on leaving town anytime soon, are you?" You see, my heart was beginning to open again, and it was scary. The wound from loving Paul so intensely in such a short span of time and then parting had built a thick wall of resistance inside me. I hung on to him for those months after we were apart because I was so intensely lonely and could not give up the notion of being in love as quickly as I took it on.

If Paul and I had stayed together the relationship would have naturally run its course...his head was in the clouds. He was sweet and I did love him for who he was, but in retrospect I believe over time he would have driven me crazy with his unrealistic way of dealing with life. What I loved were his words and his romance. But words and romance are short-lived when faced with reality.

On the other hand a heart in a shell does not open again overnight. Larry, you know that. You saw how the months went by before I said, "I love you." It's been a year now. Gee wiz, I'm even a Buddhist now. And I love you. You don't come on strong with words and romance, you're just yourself, but when faced with reality, that is everlasting. I love you Larry. Can't wait to see what the next year brings.

*   *   *

AJB:

<u>Letter to Mom, (Celeste Rose)</u>

May 4, 1988.

Hi Mom, Happy Mothers' Day! I've been painting and packing and going crazy – but I'm excited. This weekend will be the big push –Rosa helped a bunch last weekend.

Good news! Larry's not a daddy! Blood test came out totally negative. (Larry's ex-wife *I'll call Kristen*) Kristen doesn't have a prayer. He should be divorced *very* soon. He is ecstatic. He's been a huge help painting. He used to do it for a living so he knows how to do it right.

I passed the entrance level Buddhist exam which was fun. I'm stressed out from moving and being impatient and bitchy, and Larry's suffering emotional backlash from fear to ecstasy in dealing with Kristen stuff so being a testy pain in the butt so we're having fun. Vacation is set for second week in August. Treat yourself good Sunday. Love ya Mom. Allyson.

*   *   *

AJB: I just really want to chant appreciation for Larry Burnett's life. As I've been seriously striving to deepen my faith lately, I've remembered him. How young and foolish I was when I dated him and how much he put up with. I might never have started this Buddhist practice if it weren't for his patience and love. I can really see now, in retrospect how special he is and I pray for his happiness.

*   *   *

I thought of Holly, my granddaughter. Perhaps she could come to Oregon to visit her Oregon relatives. Now I had money. From Allyson's death, I had money. Looking out my window at the pine tree I decided that I would use, generously, this windfall to reach Holly.   Following that line of thought, I made plans to bring Holly and my son Max out to visit Oregon, perhaps in the summer of 1992 for the family 4th of July party.

*   *   *

Bonnie, my friend from church choir, called.   "I want to do something for you. I love you and I feel so sorry for your suffering, please let me do something to help."   Bonnie was my musician friend and colleague from Rose Children's Theatre and my church choir buddy.

"I would like that, really. I think, what I would like… I'd like you to come to me at bed time and listen to my sad story, sing to me and tuck me in."   My own elderly mother didn't do these kinds of touch-feely things.

"I'll be there."   Bonnie answered.   Afterwards Bonnie would tell me that she was scared to be so close to me. She thought. *Oh my God. I don't know how to listen to Celeste's story. It sounds really scary to be with her in her bedroom and be near so much raw grief, but I love her and I will be brave and do what she has asked me to do.*

Bonnie came at bedtime. We went to my room. I wore a nice nightgown in honor of having a visitor. I had two or three large handkerchiefs with me.   I believe that I was still sleeping with Allyson's bathrobe and teddy bear. Bonnie sat with me on the velvet patchwork comforter, looked into my eyes, and prepared to listen. "Tell me your sad story."

So I told her about cleaning Allyson's apartment and about the funeral home and seeing her body and all about Allyson turning into an orchid. I cried and Bonnie cried in sympathy. We used the large handkerchiefs.

"Now what?"

"Tuck me into bed and sing to me."

"Come on honey," said Bonnie and she pulled the covers back as I slipped my legs in between the cool sheets and lay my gray head on the pillow. She stroked my forehead and I cried into my cowboy bandana. She sat next to me and sang a lullaby, a song that her mom had sung to her when she was little, just like Roddy McDowall's mother when he thought *My Friend Flicka* was going to die.

> Another day is through,
> So go to sleep, my little Buckaroo.

Bonnie kissed my cheek goodnight, turned out the light, went down the stairs and let herself out.

It is so hard to be alone. If something like this would happen, I would go to Allyson to have her comfort me. But Allyson is the one who has died. I could go to Rosa, but she lives in another state. My elderly mother does not like to see me cry. She does the best she can, but she mainly lives in Egypt near De-Nile and wants this not to have happened. Bonnie gave me a special gift of sympathy and nurturing.

Bonnie's new husband, Paul Guthmuller, our choir director, was planning to have us all sing a Mozart Requiem. He set up an adult education class after church to meet and talk about funeral masses and sacred works of music in honor of the dead. Our assignment this week had been to write our own lament.

Lament of a Mother's Grief

By: Celeste Rose, 1992.
To: Allyson Jean Bennett, Born Jan. 3, 1964 and died April 20, 1991.

> Divine Power, unknowable force,
> Called God, *Yahweh,* Goddess, Creator.
>
> My heart is broken.
> My life of happiness is over.
> My veins run with lead.
> My head is bent. My step is slow.
>
> All seeing eye of Divine,
> All comforting arms of love,
> Many are those that have been comforted...

Take me into a sleep of forgetfulness,
Ask me into a dance of relief,
Show me one small way
That I can live through one moment of this suffering.

Show me a flower and let me remember beauty.
Play me a song and let me remember joy.
Bring one human face that can look on me with love,
A face that I can dare to love in return.
Show me some way that I can live past this goodbye,
This too-soon parting.

Thank you for this deep and profound gift of love.
The love I have for my best departed.
It is through this human love
That I experience a hint of the Divine.
Thank you for this spring day,
Though the flowers are too beautiful to be endured.
I will break from the loveliness of this music.

I am broken, I am undone,
And yet Divine love is sent
To pick me up and cradle me in patient arms.

*　　　　　*　　　　　*

There were couples in our Wednesday grief support group at
Sacred Heart. Some of these couples had suffered from loss of a child.
At the group the categories were: Loss of a child, loss of a parent,
loss of a spouse. One woman spoke of the loss of her parakeet. The
bird was her main companion.

Marcia Hilton speaks out with instructions for the session.
"Loss of a child group, meet in the counseling room by the hall. Loss
of parents? How many do we have? Raise your hand if you've lost a
parent. You meet in the library. Loss of a spouse stay here, you can
meet in that corner over there."

I felt jealous of the couples because they had each other and I seemingly had no one. There was one solid Catholic couple that had been married for more than twenty years. I thought, *this woman is not alone because she has her husband.*

Their son had been killed in an auto crash. He was a good youth, a good citizen, not the kind to run around wildly in the middle of the night driving fast cars. He drove a simple, lightweight gray Corolla. He was returning late at night after working an evening shift, driving on the Beltline, when he was hit head-on by a car driven by an old man, a ditsy elder who had lost his bearings, crossed the median and hit the young man's car and killed him. A policeman knocked on the couple's door after midnight, reporting the news.

They had only the one son, and even though they had each other, what I noticed was that the man had put his own grief aside and was *being strong* for his wife. He was allowing her to grieve and to lean on him. She was thoroughly destroyed by the death of her son.

The couple began to fall apart. He had lost his son also and his wife was not there for him. He backed off. Therefore she lost her son and her husband. So even though each half of this couple was not alone, because they had each other and they were committed partners, nevertheless everyone has different ways and different timing for their grief. The lesson for me was that when we mourn, we mourn alone.

Another woman, whose son died, had to quit the family business. She and her husband got a divorce, and the other sons went about their various tasks without paying any attention to her. Their attitude was, "Get over it." I guess being in mourning is not an attractive way to greet the public. No one wants to be around a gloomy person.

Mary Davidson, my Godsons' mother, said something very strange to me. "This is very weird, but I'll say it anyway. Because of the way you are crying for Allyson, I can see that you loved her very much. I am jealous of your depth of love for your daughter. I wish that I could experience the depth of feeling that you have at this time."

Some people are uncomfortable around raw emotion. On the other hand, people in general are fascinated with mourning, death,

killing, grief, and blood. Traffic slows down so people can get a look
at the crumpled cars in a highway accident. There are many books,
plays, movies about dead children, dying people, saying good-bye,
and a lot of songs about separation.

In some countries there is a lot more death in everyday life,
and there are systems in place to handle the bereft. Maybe a hundred
years ago, children were being born at home in the bedroom. My
ancestor Mary McMurray Maxwell, had 15 children, and only 5 or 6
made it to adulthood. The little caskets made yearly parades out of
the door and to the Lorton Cross Cemetery in Cockermouth, England.

I am resentful of modern methods. When Allyson died I
wanted to hold her, I wanted my family and me to lift her onto the
dining room table to wash and dress her. I wanted to prepare her for
burial. I would consider it a privilege. It could have been a last act of
love.

I believe that there are some Jewish rituals that require guards
or keepers to sit with the body, never leaving the corpse unattended.
The deceased might be placed on a slant board. Water is poured over
the body: maybe herbs, oils, and spices are used to anoint. There is
no embalming, and the deceased is buried quickly beneath the earth in
a simple casket or a winding sheet. After a speedy burial, members of
the community sit *shiva* for seven days. I like the tradition of sitting
shiva. I like the fact that the mourners are never left alone. The
mirrors are covered in the *shiva* house because there are prayers being
said and the mourners should not face a mirror when praying. I like
the idea of tearing one's clothes or the rabbi tearing black cloth which
is pinned to the grieving person's garments.

Women in mourning used to wear black. Men used to have
black armbands. These customs were observed for one year. A
black-ribboned wreath was placed on the front door. The neighbors
were thereby informed.

When my stepbrother and his family died in the murder-
suicide, I was living in North Carolina, far from my family. None of
my local friends knew what had happened. No one knew of this big
horrible event that affected me so deeply. When it came time for me
to call my mother and stepfather I crawled under our kitchen desk and

refused to come out. I believe that I was around twenty-six years old at that time. My husband telephoned Collins Kilburn, our preacher, and he sat with me and counseled me.

In some ancient cultures the emotion of grief was physicalized by a person cutting their hair. In my case I let my hair grow, long, unwashed and stringy. I bought another gray felt hat that I would wear with the brim up or down. I had a piece of black lace. Sometimes when I was alone, I wore the brim of the hat down and the black lace over my face. It was my *make the world go away* costume. When I was in public I tucked the black lace around my neck under my shirt or I carried it folded in my pocket.

*   *   *

My renter Suzette had been unable to separate her emotions from my grieving, and it seemed as if she waited at home to ambush me every Wednesday after my Grief Support Group. The meetings were useful for processing my feelings and hearing the stories of others who were suffering but I always felt worse when I came home--shaky, hungry, dizzy. I would enter the house and come into the kitchen and there would be Suzette waiting to argue with me or as she would say, wanting to talk our problems out. She had a nasal and puffy tone to her voice and when she was angry she sometimes sounded like a mad bull. "Celeste, you know what David did? He used my tea-towel!"

"Don't give me any problems right now, Suzette, I'm not feeling well. You know on Wednesdays I have this group counseling session and I'm trying to handle a lot of feelings."

"And another thing, I just want to know what you're going to do about this broken cupboard door. Every time I try to get a pan from under the stove the door hangs crooked. And David is using the tea-towels for gross wipe-ups. These are special embroidered tea-towels from Aunt Jane."

"Suzette, I'm not feeling up to a long discussion about cupboard doors and tea-towels. Perhaps tomorrow we can talk. I'll find my drill and some screws and bleach for the towels, and we can fix things."

"Aunt Jane is my favorite aunt, you know, from Los Angeles. I don't know why people can't just leave my things alone."

Me: "Damn it! Leave me alone, Suzette, leave me alone. I can't take this right now. I feel like I'm going to throw up!" I screamed, gasping and sobbing.

Her: "Celeste, quit being so dramatic. God, I just wanted to process some things. I thought you liked to talk things out."

Me to myself: *How can I not be dramatic? Celeste is dramatic, that's what I am. Me not being dramatic is like a snail without a shell. Like a Pacific Northwest slug.*

So the next week, we had a meeting where we really talked things out. Even though she was spiritual and a supposed counselor, she could not tolerate the way I ran the household. "Someone has to be in charge. It's your house. You're supposed to be taking care of things."

I'm thinking, *Yes and when you were a teen-ager you were the oldest of nine children, and your Dad was supposed to take care of things, your mother was sick, in fact she had epilepsy, and you had a love-hate relationship with the power he gave you over the house.* What I said was, "You've got thirty days to find another place to live. I love you and have appreciated your wisdom and friendship, but we have different ways of running things and this is my house."

About George

I had a great many problems getting along with my stepfather, George. I told Mother. "I just can't come over and talk to George right now. I'm so tender and vulnerable. I can't hardly be around him."

"That's all right," she said, "I understand. Sometimes I can't stand to be around him either."

I didn't know that he would *miss* me, but he became angry about my ignoring him. He was naggingly rude to Mother on this subject.

In 1986 a counselor told me that I was a survivor of incest. Even though George never *got me,* he had lurked about, coped a feel, stolen an adult kiss, and one time he ripped the hook-and-eye-lock off my door when I tried to install some security. The counselor explained to me, "You don't have to be penetrated for it to be incest, Celeste. For ten years you were not safe in your childhood home."

I replied, "I remember always having my radar operating when he was home: his boot steps in the hallway, in the kitchen fixing his lunch pail , getting a drink of whiskey, footsteps passing my door, closing the back door, starting the pick-up truck, driving off. Then I would relax, and know that I was safe for the day.

If he smiled at me and cocked his head, I would be terrified. Better he would be mean, but when he was nice, "Watch out!" He would back me into a corner and sweetly speak vile words to me, "What do you let the boys do to you? You let them touch you? Huh? Huh?" Sometimes he pushed against me, he didn't dare to touch me, but he breathed his whiskey breath on me and he smelled of Aqua Velva.

The era of the Fifties was a time that these behaviors were kept secret-- especially from the mothers. I told Mother's friend Edie Marshall, but she said, "He's just trying to be nice." This, then, is what I mean by "not getting along with George."

My niece Martha came to Mother's house and I wanted to go over there to see her. Mother called me. She was crying. "George says that you are not welcome in this house. I don't want you to come; you'll cause trouble."

It was time that I did something about the dis-ease of the family. I said, "I'll be right over." Martha was not there when I arrived. I went straight to George's chair. " I want to talk to you," I said.

He said, "I want to talk to you too." Or actually more like, "You got that God-damned right!"

I pulled up a chair for a *tete a tete* or as they say in Italian a *quatra occhi*, four eyes. Mother became terrified. She hated for us to fight. "No, no," she yelled. "Don't cause trouble."

I said, "Mother, George and I have something to discuss. Please leave us alone."

"Oh dear, oh dear." Mother went into the kitchen, which was right around the wall and in easy hearing distance.

"George, Allyson's death has disturbed me terribly and I am having trouble being around people, trouble with my relationships."

"You? You? You lost one child. I lost three!" He showed me with his fingers, "Three, three." He was referring to the murder-suicide that took place almost thirty years ago in 1965 when Army man, George, Jr., called Georgie, was married to a German woman, Linda. They had adopted Denise, a German baby. At the time of her death the baby was two years old. A week before the three shots were fired, Georgie had called my mother from the Louisiana Army base. "Linda and I are having a really tough time, I wonder if you and Dad could take Denise? We're not doing well and we might be heading for divorce or something."

Mother answered him. "You children will have to work things out for yourselves. I think it would be a good idea if you went to the Army chaplain and if you could get counseling or couples counseling down there."

Sometime in the next two weeks Georgie did the deed. Using a rifle, he shot Linda, then Denise and then himself. The three caskets were shipped by rail to Eugene, accompanied by an honor guard. I was living in North Carolina at the time and in my mind's eye I could visualize the sad procession: the journey in the baggage car with the caskets; then the hearses carrying the bodies from the railroad station south along Willamette Street. They were buried in Eugene at the Sunset Hills Cemetery.

Every year since then Mother cried over their graves on Memorial Day. Holding a sad bouquet from her garden, Mother would speak with tears in her voice. "Red, white and blue because he was a soldier, then I always use pink flowers for Linda and Denise. Oh, I can't help feeling guilty. They called me. They asked for help. I didn't listen. I told them to get counseling. Wasn't that the right answer? If I had taken the child, then maybe it would have relieved the tension. I could have stopped it."

Our stepfather had not been allowed to hit my brothers and me, so Georgie became the whipping boy. He had taken all our beatings during our teenaged years. I thought, *It was you, George, my grim substitute parent, it was you that loaded that rifle, you programmed those deaths.*

I looked into my angry stepparent's eyes. I said, "We each have lost children. You should understand my feelings then. I'm having a very difficult summer. I'm working and doing my tours and at the same time I feel really depressed."

George balled up his fist, and pounded his chest over his heart. "You, you just lost one. I lost my grandchild. I hurt here." He did not acknowledge my new grief. He just kept talking about what he had lost.

Mother kept popping into the living room, trying to hold off a knock-down-drag- out-fight.   I leaned over George's chair and hugged him, even kissing him on his mouth, a very cautious, thin-mouthed kiss. From then until his death I made myself visit him two times a month. These visits kept him more or less quiet so that he would not torture Mother with rantings and criticisms, "That fat lazy no-good…come over and get off her fat butt to do something around the house …doesn't give a fat-assed damn about anyone…"

Twice a month, I kissed him as a power gesture, "pissed on his leg," someone said to me. I found that a person can learn a lot from a kiss on the mouth. Some days it was dry and hot, other times, wet and cold, but this kiss was a bitter pill for me to swallow. *Did he kiss me back? I don't think so, but he lifted his face to me.*

*   *   *

From my mother, Phyllis Murray.   12 – 21 – 91
Dear Celeste,
I'll write you a love letter while I'm baking cookies for Sally's harp students' party. I do love you and miss you at this time especially. When you are in town I don't feel so alone.
George said he was sorry he caused a fuss and said he would try not to do it again. I hope it won't keep you from coming to see

me. However, I wouldn't blame you if you never darkened our door again. He is a sick man and now that he is almost blind I have a feeling of compassion for him. I forgive him 365 days a year. He does not think before he speaks and often says. "I didn't mean it the way it sounded."

Well, so much for that! Excuse me while I get a pan of cookies out of the oven. (To be continued.) I got the pan a little too brown so we will eat it. My stove timer is hard to set. I want to buy a little one to use that is easier.

Christmas cards pouring in now. I enjoy them.

Winston just called. They are going to stop by on their way out to the coast. Well, I better stop or you won't have time to read my rambling letter.

I'm saving enough cookies to take each of my good neighbors a plate. Will also share some of the fruitcake Maxwell sent. Loads of love and kisses to everyone there.

I love all very much. Mother

P.S. I give fruit to my diabetics next door.

My stepfather, George Murray, died in January 8, 1995, and according to Mother, he wanted to be embalmed and laid in a casket, then be buried at Sunset Hills next to his son, daughter-in-law, and grandchild Denise.

I demanded a formal visitation at the funeral home: open casket, the corpse in full make-up and dress suit displayed in a quiet, beautiful room.

On viewing day I entered the room at Poole Larsen Funeral Home, bringing from home a small bottle of bourbon, and pulled up a chair. The cosmetologist had done a wonderful job with his face. He had a faint smile on his lips; he was pink and healthy- looking, not the cold, sweating man I knew always sitting in his lounge chair. This time I did not have to kiss his mouth. I sat next to him and put my right hand on his chest and patted the corpse.

I took a swig of whisky and spoke. "What was all this about? You wanted a daughter, I wanted a father, but you had to be, in your words, a horse's ass. Me? I had to protect myself from you for fifty years, always watching after my own, in my words, *beautiful* ass. Why couldn't you have been nice? Look at you now, you seem like such a nice fellow, a friendly smile there." I took another swig from the bottle.

At this point Martha and her husband Glenn walked in. She saw me with the bottle, sitting next to the casket. "Aunt Celeste!" She laughed.

"Yes, I'm just having a very pleasant talk with George. He's so easy to talk to, no griping or complaining."

"He does look nice, that's for sure."

She came closer. I stood and moved my chair back. She said, "We just wanted to pay our respects."

I said, "I wanted to be sure he was really dead."

Mother, age almost 86, was getting a little bit feeble and she let me take charge of the arrangements. I guess I'll go ahead and put down what I did next. I admit I was glad to have the old guy out of my life. The phrase *dancing on his grave* comes to mind.

First, I ordered a blue denim-covered metal casket in honor of his love of all things cowboy. Plus it was one of the cheaper choices. I had them put a bolo tie at the collar of his shirt. I ordered his Stetson hat to be included on top the casket. Then I had a genius thought. *I'll order an honor guard, a cowboy in western regalia to walk the path at the cemetery.*

I called a horse-birthday-party rental. "Would you come to a funeral with your horse?"

"We've never done anything like that, but I suppose we could do that."

"What do you charge, say, for a birthday party?"

"Seventy-five dollars per hour. I guess we'd charge the same for a memorial service."

I organized the horse and rider, asking them to use an ornate western saddle with the rider in full western dress with cowboy hat. He was to wait behind the mausoleum until a particular time. "I want you to ride slowly down the access road toward my step-father's graveside." We were all to be seated under an awning. I told no one except my preacher brother.

At the chosen time we heard the clip-clop of the horse and everyone turned their eyes toward the sound. Mother said, "A horse! Oh a horse."

People burst into tears, accompanied with massive nose-snuffling. The rider turned to George's open grave with denim casket there and the cowboy hat on top the box. He came to the edge and dismounted, urged the horse under the tent, then tapped the animal's front leg. The horse made a bow. The cowboy removed his own hat and said the words that I had given him, "So long, partner." More weeping.

Everyone sat there; eyes bugged out. I thought to myself, *Well, honestly, the only time I ever really loved this man was the time that he borrowed a palomino horse and, dressed in cowboy casual, rode to my mother's house to come courting.* This visit naturally impressed us three kids. "Marry him, Mommy. Marry him." We chimed.

The cowboy walked up to the casket and laid a bouquet of *dendrobium* orchids, Allyson's flowers, on the casket. He returned to the horse, heaving himself into the saddle, turned the horse and rode away. The orchids, not the prickly rose, were to be the flowers from my daughter, the peace child.

$$*\qquad\qquad*\qquad\qquad*$$

Rosa said that she was coming to see me. When she called to cancel her plans, I broke down. My usual answer to disappointment would have been, "That's OK, just do what's best for you." In my delicate condition I was unable to withstand any problems. I was bluntly honest with people. My defenses were down, I could not put on a happy face. I cried out, "I have been waiting for you. I need you so very much, I cannot stand it if you do not come."

Rosa came in August. We opened up the box of Allyson's ashes. They were pretty and sparkly. When questioned, the man at the funeral home explained to me, "The ashes are not really ashes. The heat of the oven consumes everything but bone. We put the bones into a pulverizer, making what we call *ashes*. It's interesting but sometimes some of the dental work survives the process. They are bones, that's why the cremains are so densely heavy."

I had talked to my friend Jerry about wanting to sprinkle the ashes far around the world. Allyson had prayed for peace at her Buddhist altar for a year before her death. I felt that perhaps her ashes were imbued with the power of peace. It was my idea to send these ashes far and wide and embrace the world with her good *Karma*.

Jerry said, "Why don't you go to one of those gift stores and get some beautiful little boxes. You can put ashes in the boxes and whenever you go anywhere, just take one or two of the little boxes along with you."

When Rosa came, we divided up the cremains into a dozen or so beautiful oval boxes that were decorated with roses and other flowers. Rosa and I dug around the dogwood tree that Mother had given me, putting some of Allyson's ashes under the roots. We also dug ashes down under the Peace Rose that Yvonne had given me.

Rosa and I drove up the McKenzie Highway to the old scenic route. We followed the steep switchback road. In August the vine maples were turning red, showing signs of autumn in the higher elevations. The ancient lava flow can be seen for miles in three directions. There are no trees, just the lava rocks. I love it up there. It is so quiet, the sun shines and the wind blows. You can see snow-capped peaks in every direction. We took a portion of Allyson's ashes to the end of the trail and I climbed a ways out onto the rocks to release the ashes into the wind. There was a cloud of gray and then she was gone. In the lava field it was literally ashes to ashes. We took a hike on Folley Ridge to Rainbow Falls overlook. I stood on a cliff overlooking a tree-filled valley. "I love you, Allyson." I yelled out as loud as I could over the empty valley. "I love you forever."

Chapter Seventeen

Like a Rosebud

Summer of 1991 Shannon moved into my rooming house. She was an eighteen-year-old freshman at the University of Oregon. She was a blessing in this year of travail. Her dad had died recently and she had grieved and had witnessed her mother's sorrow. She was not afraid of my tears or of my dramatic fits. She gave me a CD from Roy Orbison, a song of the pain of parting, "In the Real World", by Kerr and Jennings. I listened to this piece over and over. His weeping voice echoed my own deep longings. "In the real world there are things that we can't change."

I returned home on a sunny day. In the car I had begun to feel anxious and upset, as if I had done something awful. I pulled into the driveway and parked my Maxima station wagon. I came in the front door and went directly out the back. Shannon, the beautiful somebody-else's daughter, lay on a blanket sunning her bikini-clad body.

"Shannon, Allyson's going to be so mad at me. I got rid of all her sandals. What's she going to do when she comes back and finds out that all her sandals are gone. She'll be so mad at me. I should have kept her sandals." I was on my knees and curled forward.

Shannon put her book down and moved to kneel beside me. Arm around my bent back, she said, "It's OK , Celeste. It'll be fine. We'll all be so happy when she comes back that we'll splurge and buy her lots and lots of sandals. It'll be so great! She can have all the expensive sandals her heart desires."

October 17th, 1991, North Carolina.

I made a visit to Raleigh, to the bosom of my dear friends, to the bosom of our shared past where my friends and I traced the path of my family. With my friends, Vann and Ramona, I started at the new Rex Hospital to see the babies in the nursery. I remembered Allyson here as a newborn. She spent her first few days in an isolette because she was so small, 4 lbs. 7 oz. Then Vann drove us to Beaver Dam Road, to the little brick house where Lawton, Max and I welcomed the swaddled infant home.

At this visit, as I stood on the top of the hill looking out at the dogwoods, poplars and pines, I could almost hear the echoes from the past--the click of the camera taking Ph.D. pictures of Lawton in his cap, gown and stole; of the sounds of Max shouting good-byes on his way triumphantly to kindergarten and first grade; of the cooing baby with the singing mom who stayed home, baking bread, visiting neighbors, breast-feeding. How the baby and I used to sit in the wicker-bottomed rocking chair, looking out at the changing seasons in the trees, the winter trees with squirrel paths, the spring trees with dogwood blossoms.

I sang, "If that mockingbird won't sing, Mama's going to buy you a diamond ring…" Baby Allyson was so tiny, so good-smelling, like a rose bud. I remembered the hours we two were together with the dog, Sandy, who shared his dog toy and his dog dish with the crawling baby in her long nightgown with the drawstring skirt, inch-worming along like Pop-eye's Sweet Pea child. The love of the young family echoed around the now empty house. I remembered the long-ago spring with the daffodil path winding down to the street below. Now autumn leaves were dried and blowing, while my twenty-five-year-old young mother's body fell away into memory like the leaves that rustled at my mature-woman's feet.

Ramona and Vann, supported me as witnesses for my grieving heart as we visited the creek where my long ago family used to play with sticks and rocks—spreading picnics and finding turtles; my son stung by yellow-jackets; Allyson the toddling baby, protected from the street by the sheltie dog bred to herd flocks. I was here to gather Raleigh memories, then to let them go like a spinner releasing the wool to be twisted into yarn. Later, I will weave these fibers into cloth for a cloak, a cloak of recovery, for I trust there will be more life to live.

From the creek, Vann and Ramona drove me across town to have lunch at Roberta Horton's house. She waited there with a warm heart—a woman who knew my daughter. The sky shone blue above and the trees were brightly autumn-colored in the neighborhood where our family spread out into larger quarters. Roberta, the weaver, with her loom, bird feeders and plastic flamingoes, welcomed me with her jolly laugh.

She and I visited the second creek—and the wonderful tree. A second-life tree. A tree that had fallen down but kept its roots, each former limb rising up to become second, third, and fourth trees, with the old trunk making magical sitting places. I remember that our beloved dog was buried here beside this creek. I reached my hand to the approximate spot to imagine stroking the warm puppy once again.

I saw the yard at the second house where we lived. The tiny trees that we had planted had grown into a forest. The boxwood plants by the street had matured into a substantial hedge. The cement work Lawton had planned, poured, and pressed with the imprint of ferns, had proudly weathered the years.

I went forward on my pilgrimage to Allyson's kindergarten teacher, Mrs. Benbow. I did not know her name was Sarah. I did not know that she had epilepsy. She and I hugged through this new connection, she from the knowledge of having epilepsy herself and finding out the little girl who used to sing Christmas carols and sell her Girl Scout cookies had died from epilepsy. Mrs. Benbow's sympathy was shared not by words but an exchange of energy.

During supper, a conversation with a woman friend revealed to me that there is more than one way to lose a child. People lose their children through drugs and alcohol, misunderstandings and anger, neglect and indifference. Now divorced, she was facing her life bereft and alone.

The next morning former singing companions Shirley and Harvey Gold and I visited Pullen Park in Raleigh. I wanted to see Allyson's favorite carrousel, now newly painted. Brassy music still played on the calliope. Standing near the swings we heard the voice of a young mother, "Allyson, come here."

Smiling, Shirley said, "That's for you, Celeste! She waited just for you to call her child's name." This made me cry. It was so sweet, so funny.

At the carrousel Raleigh's other little Allyson child came with her mother to get on a horse and hold tight. Harvey, wearing a reddish-tan broad-brimmed hat, sat on a horse of the same color, gilded with gold. I rode a dapple gray, because it is a circus horse. My horse had an open mouth with teeth showing, its eyes slightly panicked—a touch of the wild but tamed by the carrousel. The ride was beautiful in the continuing perfect weather. The three singers, recognizing the songs on the calliope, sang along.

I remembered Allyson at the doctor's office where she always screamed for no reason. I explained to her, " I promise that we'll go to Pullen Park if you do not cry this time."

I remembered my son Maxwell holding Allyson's hand and saying to her, "Allyson, don't cry at the doctor's because then we can go ride on the horses at the merry-go-round."

I visited Robert and later his mother, Franka, my old neighbor and Italian friend. What could be said? Robert was dying of AIDs. He said, "I am ready to die." He told me that he continued to go to work every day.

I said, "But why go to work if you are dying?"

He answered, "I like my work. I want to just keep living a normal life."

I hoped that what he said was true. His mother Franka lived with the sure knowledge of her son's early death. Her heart was broken like mine, but broken every day with the dread of the impending disaster to her family. She talked at great length about her papa. She loved him best. I was secretly jealous that she had a long life with her father. I had no father, no grandfather. She told me that upon his death they glued his mouth shut. People remember such gruesome details! Her brother also had died young. Now she waited with her son for his sure death.

Franka remembered Allyson, but mostly she remembered Max as a baby. Her family lived next door to us and she would babysit. When he cried, she clutched him mightily to her breast, rocked *furiuoso,* and sang opera arias loudly in her tenor range. Later, when granddaughter Holly met Franka, she said, "That is the most interesting woman I have ever met."

I said, "Holly, Franka is an Italian, and there is a whole country full of those kinds of people. When you are in high school, I will take you to Italy."

Saturday night the old "Cradle-rockers" group joined for singing. When we began singing together in 1964 we were all young couples with babies and children. I was the guitar teacher, the "Mama Cass," for many of the musicians. During this visit we remembered the harmonies for our old familiar songs. When Harvey sang, with his basso voice, the song about "The Traveling People," I curled up on the floor close to him, so that the vibrations of his voice and the nostalgia of the words could wash over me.

<u>Freeborn Man of the Traveling People</u>
By Ewan MacColl
Then we'd pack our load and be on the road
They were good old times for the R-0-V-E-R.

The various members of the group held me and hugged me. How good it felt. *How could something so sad and so terrible feel so good?*

We ended the weekend with a little mini-memorial service, a weekend among friends on the occasion of grieving for my dead daughter, a weekend bittersweet and perfect, a sad ballad played on a gut-string guitar against the smooth velvet background of a North Carolina twilight. I lifted my voice to close the evening, "Thank you, Spirit, for letting me come here, for these friends gathered. I thank you for helping me to remember Allyson--the little baby, the child, the woman."

Chapter Eighteen

"Hi Grandma, It's Me Holly"

Autumn of 1993, Allyson's cousin Anne Maxwell married Mike Hammond. Another cousin, Martha Maxwell, married Glenn Griffith. My reaction to these much celebrated events was a deep longing for the life that Allyson did not get to live. No marriage for her. No future. No children. I was agonizingly jealous. What could I add to the experiences that she would miss? I thought, *she will never have a fortieth birthday party.*

Martha and Glenn chose an outdoor space for their marriage ceremony, a wedding garden out River Road toward Junction City. It was October, but still almost mild enough. It didn't rain. There were harp solos because all those girl Maxwells play harp. There was a fanfare of horns because Glenn plays trombone. The reception took place inside a heated building with tables, chairs, decorations, cake, champagne, and food.

I talked to Mrs. King. She had been neighbors of the Maxwells all these years. I was in choir with her son, David King, who died the summer of 1957 after our graduation from South Eugene High School. That June, dark-haired, olive-skinned, smiling David, so gracious and polite, died of a brain tumor. "Mrs. King, I am Celeste Rose. I went to school with your David."

"Oh yes, I remember you, of course."

"We have something sad in common with one another."

"Yes, what is that, dear?"

"I have a child that died young, well as a young adult. Her name was Allyson, and she died when she was 27."

"Oh, I'm sorry to hear that. It's so sad when they die young." She smiled at me and her eyes sparkled.

"David was a good person."

"Yes, he was a wonderful son. I am so glad I had him for those eighteen years. He was my only child, but he was a really good one. I'm a lucky person."

I thought. *Loving with all your heart is a dangerous act. The vulnerable heart is easily wounded, but better to have loved and lost. It is a good thing to really really love.*

I heard a champagne cork pop and the inevitable laughter that follows the splash of wine. I shuttled behind a partition and wiped my eyes and nose. I was jealous of these weddings, these celebrations of young womanhood. I had to change my attitude. To this purpose I discovered a cure: *Think of a recipe for potato salad.* It is impossible to get emotional about the recipe for potato salad.

I went out to get some champagne, to laugh and celebrate. "Isn't the dress beautiful!"

"Yes, but we were so cold."

"Lucky guys, they all get to wear tuxedoes."

I think: *Cut into cubes the chilled cooked potatoes and add a handful of bread-and-butter pickle pieces. Chop celery, chop boiled eggs, and mix together. Olives are good. Mayonnaise with a lump of mustard, then the secret ingredient.* "Yes, I have a son. His name is Max and he lives in Texas." *Lump of Mustard.* "What? Oh, Texarkana, Texas. He has a child, Holly Bennett. Oh, I am lucky. I enjoy my granddaughter so much, though I am far away. I discipline myself to write her a letter once a month. It's better than the telephone, really. She can collect the letters and put them in a special box. She can keep the envelopes full of hand-written letters with love and kisses marked on the bottom. She can hold them in her hands."

"Does she write you?"

"Yes, I collect her letters to me. I remember some of those wonderful childish letters. *Grandma, It's me, Holly.*

*   *   *

Holly's letters at six and seven years old.

NOV. 21, 1987
DEAR GRANDMA, HOW ARE YOU DOING? HAVE YOU HAD ANY
SHOWS YET? I WENT TO A BIRTHDAY PAR – TY LAST NIGHT. I
WAS BIG BIRD ON
HALLOWEEN. PAGE 2 MY DAD AND I WENT TO A HALLOWEEN
CARNIVAL. SCHOOL IS FUN, I AM GETTING GOOD GRADES IN
SCHOOL. MY TEACHER'S NAME IS MRS. GENTRY.
I AM A MONKEY FAN. NOW I AM GOING TO FIRST GRADE
SUNDAY SCHOOL AND I AM GOING TO CHOIR TOO. I AM
GOING TO HAVE A BIRTHDAY PARTY AT MCDO –
NOLD'S. I HOPE YOU HAVE A HAPPY THANKSGIVING. LOVE
HOLLEY P.S. DAD AND I WROTE THIS LETTER. XXX000

4 – 30 – 88
DEAR GRANDMA, HI, IT'S ME HOLLY. HOW DO I SPELL MY
NAME. WELL, HOLLY OR HOLLEY WILL DO. I THINK YOU
WANTED ME TO SEND YOU THE FEATHER BACK. I SENT IT
BACK BUT WILL YOU PLEASE SEND IT BACK TO ME TO KEEP. I
LOVE THE COLOR PINK.
                              PAGE 2
        WHERE DID YOU GET THAT FEATHER ANYWAY. THAT
COLOR I SENT YOU IT WAS SKY BLUE, BUT WHAT DOES
TURGUISE MEEN, WRITE ME AND TELL ME. I HAVE GOT A GIFT
FOR YOU IN THE THING GO TO PAGE THREE. I HAVE GOT A
SURPRISE FOR YOU. (GAMES, GAMES)
I HOPE YOU HAVE FUN DOING THE GAMES. LOVE YOUR
LOVING GRANDAUGHTER HOLLY
P.S. SEND THE GAMES BACK SO I CAN CHECK THEM.

DATE UNKNOWN
DEAR GRANDMOTHER, HI IT'S ME HOLLEY. I AM GOING TO
BIBLE SCHOOL ...YOU NOW WHAT, YOU NOW PUFF THE MAGIC
DRAGON, WELL, I HAVE GOT A DOLL OF HIM. HERE IS A
COLOR, CUT IT OUT AND SEND IT BACK WITH IT'S NAME. CUT
ALONG THE DOTTED LINE. YOU NOW HOW MUCH MONEY I
HAVE GOT? 3.05 IN MY BANK. I AM STARTING A CLUB. IT'S
CALLED THE SECRET KIDS. I'M ALSO IN BROWNIE GIRL
SCOUTS.
YOU NO WHEN YOU SENT ME A LETTER A FEW DAYS AGO?
WELL YOU WROTE GIVE MAX AND NAYNCIE A HUG.

INSTEAD, BUT I DON'T MIND. I NOW WHY YOU PUT O FOR KISSES AND X FOR HUGS. YOU PLACE YOUR LIPS IN AN O SHAPE WHEN YOU KISS, AND WHEN YOU HUG YOU CROSS HEADS.
MY SCHOOL GETS OUT ON JULY 1 FRIDAY NOT REALLY, BUT I WANT YOU TO BE ABLE TO PLAY YOU NOW WHAT. ["You know what" is a game of Gingerbread man where Holly runs and runs.]
WHEN THE BOY PUSHED ME DOWN A FEW DAYS AGO, IT MADE A SCRATCH ON MY BRIDGE. LOVE HOLLEY XXXOOO

Letter from Oregon (I sent a word game.)
Dear Holly,
You can send this back to me. I am sending an envelope for you to use.
Sorry but "X" stands for kiss and "O" stands for hug. "O" is hug because your arms go around and "X" for kiss because it sounds like smacking. I love you. XXXOOOO Grandma Celeste.

MAE 4 [Meaning May 4 but her middle name is Mae.]
HI, IT'S ME HOLLY, I GOT YOUR
LETTER, CELESTE ROSE! WHAT'S
HAPPENED TO YOUR NAME! I WILL
TELL YOU THE ANSERS TO ALL THOSE GAMES. WHEN YOU VISIT ME.
BOTH OF THE TESTS WE HAD?
(TEAMS A CAT?) I MADE THE HIGHEST SCORE THERE WAS.
LOVE HOLLY XXXOOO

1988
DEAR GRANDMA,
ARE YOU STILL COMING FOR THE SUMMER? IF YOU ARE, BRING ME A PRESENT PLEASE.
WE CAN HAVE A PUPPET SHOW WITH TICKETS, AND I CAN INVITE MY FRIEND'S TO WATCH IT, WE COULD HAVE A LEMONADE STAND WITH COOKIES TO. LEMONADE 10 c COOKIES 5 c. LOVE HOLLY

4-4-88
DEAR GRANDMA, IT'S ME HOLLEY. I HOPE YOU HAVE GOT MY EASTER CARD. I HOPE YOU CAN COME TO VISIT ME THIS SUMMER. IF YOU CAN COME THIS SUMMER, DO YOU REMEMBER MY AUNT CYB WELL WE CAN SWIM IN HER POOL. LOVE, HOLLEY

Holly is 13 years old. 1994 she writes on letterhead stationery from her Perkins Grannie's antique shop.

<u>Whitaker House Antiques</u>

Dear Grandma,
     I'm typing on my new electric typewriter. This is cool! How is everybody? We're fine here. Next Saturday is U.I. L. I'm competing in spelling and writing. Wish me luck! I've been studying like crazy to get ready for spelling. For writing there's not much I can do except pray! Don't worry, I do know how to type. Mrs. Everhart made the whole class take the typing lessons on the computer. But I will say this: I'm going to need to replace the correction tape very soon. I'm doing alien abduction for my science project this year, and it's turned out to be a lot more intriguing than I expected. I'm partners with my friend Melissa. I've had all straight A's all year. Yeah! I think I'll be able to keep it up. (I hope I can, anyway) How was your Valentine's Day? Mine was good. I got 2 candy grams at school. (You order them from student council for a dollar to send to anyone, and they're delivered 6th period) One came from my P.S. teacher and the other from my friend Misty. I also sent her one. You should remember her – she came with us [swimming] to Crystal Springs and helped us paint. [We painted Holly's bedroom upstairs at Whitaker House.] Well, that's all I've got to say for now. Write back soon! Love. Holly Bennett, granddaughter.

*   *   *

I continue talking to Mrs. King at Martha and Glenn's wedding. "She also has learned to write me on her own. Not every month, but several times a year. She sends me pictures that she draws. Or her dad draws pictures for me. I see her every other year or so. Next summer she is coming to Oregon to visit. We both love to swim.

"I bought stationery with graphics of puppies and kitties on it. She would bounce out to the mailbox and see at a glance if she'd received a letter from her Oregon Grandmother. The funniest thing is when she was really little. I had to fashion long chatty letters that would keep her interest. I didn't mention my colonoscopy or my trip to the gym. I didn't talk about the books I was reading or exchange recipes. I told her about the squirrels in our yard and the homeless cats. I told her about my Halloween costume and that I was afraid of funny food. I couldn't mention that I was terrified of dentists because that might mark her for life. I did talk about playing guitar and singing with a group at the long folklore weekends."

*   *   *

Every October In Eugene, my friends and I like to go to the Hilton Hotel lobby for the Halloween street parade. We don't go to the dance inside the ballroom, which costs money, but we like to dress up and hang out in the lobby and watch the arrivals of the people in costumes. One year I was a chicken, then a friendly dinosaur, when Bart and I went, he was a tree and I was a fat wood-numph, ha ha, that's about right, a wood-numph not a wood-nymph.

The Halloween during my travel through tragedy I decided to really go dark. Something Allyson would have appreciated. I dressed as a baby-sitter from hell: gray uniform, white apron with blood stains, a nurse's cap, with the words "Loving care baby sitting service." I had a really scary rubber mask--wounds and pus running down the face. I carried a "dead" baby. I put comic kind of ex-es over the baby doll's eyes. The costume was so awful. People held their hands up and fled from me.

I stumbled in my blood-spotted shoes, carrying my blanket-wrapped "dead" baby and walked toward the other people, mumbling, "Come to me, I will take good care of you. Come to me."

Especially the women screamed, "Get away from me. Oh my God."

There were two big gutsy boys from The Rose Children's Theatre, Linda Frobach's children, and I saw them in the crowd, so I took my horror-nanny over to them and said, "Come with me."

These boys, who were never afraid of anything, registered terror, screamed maniacally and ran away. Part of the evening I sat on the steps and rocked my dead baby and moaned. It was the true spirit of Halloween. It felt good to be so blatant with my suffering and because of the mask to be anonymous at the same time.

Since that time I have celebrated every year the Day of the Dead. I bought a fun Allyson skeleton in a bikini that has a boom box. I put out a dish of chocolates for Allyson. I have her picture there, my dad's picture, and for George, my stepfather, I put an open can of beer on the front porch, so that he would not come in. I decorated the room with skeletons and flowers.

Rosa called. "The veil is thin this time of year, the veil between those who are alive and those who are dead."

I agreed, "I'm always hoping that I'll have an Allyson dream. It's so weird that I don't see her in my dreams."

I finally did have a few dreams of Allyson. *Oh joy, to be visited after such a long time apart.* She sitting on a washing machine at a laundromat. She sat with her legs hanging down and thumped the side of the metal box with the heels of her sneakers. Her voice was happy and excited, "Mom, I have something important to tell you."

I yelled with such enthusiasm. "Allyson!" This scream woke me up and Allyson and her news disappeared. *Aargh! What was the news? News from the other side? What was it?*

Another rare dream, a long and complicated dream: cars, no roads, scenery like Roman ruins, cement pieces to drive around, vines growing over rocks, down the hillsides. Allyson is driving the car and I am sitting in the back seat. I feel frustrated that I'm not driving. Where is she taking me? "Watch out where you're going." I say.

She drives a little too fast, a lot out of control, bouncing over large rocks, swerving around great slabs of cement. She's driving, she's in control, I am a passenger and I am not happy.

*   *   *

For the Christmas season I moved to my brother's house in Vancouver, Washington because I had a 40 day job in the Portland area, hand puppet shows, four each evening, at the Festival of Lights at the Grotto.   The Grotto, 82nd and Sandy in Portland, has a monastery, a chapel, and landscaped garden that at Christmas displays millions of lights emphasizing the story of Jesus. In the chapel there are four choirs per night, 120 plus choirs: church, community, and school choirs, singing Christmas music, making the event the largest choir festival in the U.S. In the plaza there is a petting zoo and my hand puppet show. At four twenty-minute shows a night, my understudy and I present more than 120 performances. The plays alternate by five year cycles but the shows repeat the same theme (everyone is worthy). Titles are: The Littlest Angel, Princess Tip Toe, The Lion and the Lamb, The Donkey's Christmas Pageant, and Star Over Africa.

Nineteen-ninety-one was different because I had to face: the first Thanksgiving, the first Christmas, the first New Year, and the first remembering of her birthday on January third, all without Allyson in my life. Between shows at the festival I hid out in the break room behind the offices. Sister Ruth found me there but she didn't talk to me, she looked at me in surprise. Even this nun didn't know what to say to a grieving mother. *Didn't she study this at sister school?*

I signed up for one-on-one counseling with one of the Grotto counseling staff. In addition to that I found a group called the Compassionate Friends in Portland. Perhaps my brother and his wife weren't thrilled with having a gloomy relative at their house for the season? I pretended to be "up" and cheerful. Sometimes this behavior works anyway,--the "paint a happy face" technique. Smiles, even the fake smiles, can add happy squirts of chemistry to your mood.

For Christmas I put a glass angel candleholder for Allyson on the mantel. I hung Allyson's personalized stocking on the fireplace. My idea was to ask people to write notes of appreciation for Allyson's life and to put these notes into her stocking.

"I am thankful for my cousin Allyson, she was a good friend to me."

"I am sorry for the loss of such a good friend."

"Missing you, remember your generosity."

"I remember the bum in the park and Allyson taking the coffee and breakfast to him and giving him a stocking full of goodies."

Then my niece Anne gave me a plaque. "Live, love, make music, be happy." The words are spelled in punched-out clay. *My God!* I couldn't stand the pain. There I was in the middle of Christmas-present-opening with this horrible cheerful plaque on my lap. I screamed, "Oh no! How can I ever be happy again!"

Anne was mortified. I had embarrassed her. And she above all members of the family had inherited my brother Farley's sensitive spirit.

At Farley's church the tradition is that the pastor's family serves cookies and punch so I showed up on the December Sunday after church with my red vest on. "Thank you, Merry Christmas," I said as I helped one after another to refreshments. There was a pink-cheeked young man, maybe seventeen years old, who said, "Thank you, Merry Christmas." I smiled and nodded at him and gave him a cookie.

"Merry Christmas." He repeated. I think he expected me to respond with "Merry Christmas to you, too." But I just smiled and nodded again. He stepped closer and took the cookie on the little paper plate. "Merry Christmas," he recapitulated between clenched teeth.

I had all I could take of holiday cheer. I tried thinking of potato salad but nothing would refocus my attention away from darkness and doom. I looked around, all was joyful, all was jubilant, all sorrows were forgotten... but not for me.

I leaned toward the sweetly-smiling young person. "As it happens, you see, I am not having a happy season. My heart is broken. We have had a tragic death in our family and I don't feel like saying, 'Merry Christmas,' so just take your juice and your cookie and go somewhere else. I'm sure someone in the room will share your joy."

His eyes wide behind his glasses, his mouth agape, he stepped back away from me. He realized that Pastor Farley Maxwell's sister was a genuine, fire breathing Scrooge with "Bah, Humbug!" Erupting from her mouth.

"Excuse me," he said and left the area.

*   *   *

There was that other long-ago Christmas at Farley's Fort Vancouver house when Allyson was alive. Everyone was there. Robin and her boyfriend Brad, Anne, Julio, Allyson, Farley and Mary, Max, Nancy and Holly from Texas, Mother and George and me-- everybody's Aunt Celeste. Farley and I decided not to do a turkey so we made Cornish game hens which we served on two beautiful round green glass platters with a wreathlike presentation, their necks to the center, and orange slices and parsley between. My daughter-in-law Nancy, (the one with the mental problems) got mad because she didn't want to eat her vegetables. She demanded a Classic Coke and a burger.

Holly, so cute and little, had disembarked from the plane wearing a white fake rabbit fur coat.

The young people gathered in the T.V. room to smoke cigarettes and my stepfather/ grandfather George went in there because he smoked cigarettes too, and he started talking inappropriate sex-talk to the teen-agers. They got grossed out and threw him out of the room.

We wouldn't let Nancy smoke cigarettes in the rest of the house, and she got mad again and called Texas to Granny Billie. "Mama, people up here are so rude. I would never be so impolite to a guest. They're just awful and I don't have any thing to eat. I'm starving."

Because of her fear of flying, she refused to go to the airport for the ride back to Texas and we were afraid that we would have to keep her. *No!* We decided to drug her. Mary is an RN but refused to find us a tranquilizer, so Farley called the people in his church to see if he could find someone with drugs to calm down this hysterical visitor long enough to get her on the plane.

Farley put on a trench coat with the collar up, went to the alley behind the Fort Vancouver house and stood next to a tree. The parishioner drove up in a dark Lexus with the drugs and Preacher Farley stepped out from behind the tree. "Have you got the stuff?"

"Here," they said. "I hope this helps."

"Thanks."

Kisses goodbye, and we hauled the Texas family into my puppet van to drive them to the airport. I hugged my little rabbit-granddaughter good-bye. Holly hugged everyone and the family parted ways again.

I remember 1985 the Christmas when Allyson and I were sleeping on an air mattress bed together in one of the rooms of the Fort Vancouver house. She liked to come home on the Christmas holidays during her college years.

I was in Eugene until the 24th working on *The Christmas Carol* with the Oregon Repertory Theatre. My van was full of wrapped presents and I was in charge of getting them up to Washington for Christmas Eve. My van broke and I had to rent a big car to get the gifts up there. Driving up to the back of the historic home, I was warmed by the bright lights shining out of the windows and the promise of a loving holiday inside.

Allyson and I talked often on the phone, and I'm a letter writer, so when we were together there was not so much new to say. But talk we did and shy Allyson was loquacious when it came to talking to her family. We used to cuddle. We played *"mothers and babies,"* a game where she sat on my lap and I rocked her.

Chapter Nineteen

New Years 1992

The year 1992 is a year that Allyson will never see. Her birthday was January third and this is the first birthday after her death. Returning from my puppeteering job in Portland, I joined the Davidsons, (that is Mary and Dale and the two godsons, Brad and Teddy) and the gang, which included friend Jason, David Stelle from my house, and Barbara Snow my sister-like friend from Eugene. It was our yearly ritual to meet up at the McKenzie River at the old bell-ringing church at Leaburg, Oregon.

We took turns ringing the bell, this year ninety-two times. The clanging sound filled the dark of the little Oregon town. The bell rope hangs down into the sanctuary. *Hold on tight and the rope lifts you off the floor.* One…Two…Three…Ninety-one (the year she died) …ninety-two…(when I go on without her.)

Barbara helped me to write a letter to Allyson and put it in a birthday card. We took the envelope (with no stamp) to the spillway by the Leaburg Dam and threw it into the foam. *Happy Birthday to Allyson from your mom.*

AJB: Journal Entry,   She writes about December 31, 1979
(singing) Last night I had the strangest dream
I dreamed the world had all agreed
To put an end to war—

Have you ever heard that song? I forgot the rest. I remember my sophomore year in high school, I felt like this, only it was worse. I was alone. It was New Years Eve and I was babysitting. Don't ever spend New Years alone—anyway I was listening to the radio and all I heard on the news was about the hostage crisis in Iran.

"…more trouble in the Middle East and Everywhere."

And I thought to myself—we're gonna go to war and nuke each other off the face of the earth and I probably won't even make it through high school. We're all gonna die, or even worse live as a mutated race. Ya know, that night I considered, for a moment, killing myself, what was the use of living or working toward goals that I knew I'd never reach before I died-- before we all died. The guy on the radio kept talking about welcoming in the 80's a new decade a decade of what? War? Death? Insanity? But it was worse then than now. Even though there is a war 'cus I'm not alone tonight. Would you please hold me? Tight? I love you…[She probably refers to Jesus Christ or a Christian God here. Unless she is thinking of her new found love, Scott, from Camp Adams.]

*   *   *

United Church of Christ, (UCC) has a yearly summer camp for high-schoolers at Camp Adams in the Cascade Mountains near Molalla, Oregon. The cousins and others in a close-knit group spent a week there together every summer, Allyson Bennett with Robin Maxwell, Farley's oldest daughter. The gang: Andrea, Michael, Jane spent a week together every year.

Finally, after everyone had given up all hope, Allyson found a boy, a love, at camp. The news went out on the family grapevine. "Allyson has a boyfriend." They thought it would never happen. She just never seemed to go in that direction. Maybe because of being shy or being very wise, she didn't fall for every Kevin, Mike, or Jason that came along.

At camp that week in June 1979, these two young Christians had been set a task. Allyson from Eugene and Scott from The Dalles had agreed to find symbols for the seven last words of Christ, the sayings from the Bible that lead up to his crucifixion. At 1:00 in the afternoon they sat next to one another at a craft table surrounded by scissors, construction paper, and marking pens. Allyson said, "We can make the sayings in balloons, like for comic books."

Scott smiled, beginning to get interested in the project. "Then we can have symbols pictured below."

She nodded, "Like for the garden, a sort of Easter lily or something. And a rooster crowing beside the Peter-betrayal-thing. The rooster could be taunting Peter."

"Or golden coins for Judas." He gestured picturing the circle of the coin. "Just like the *Magic Penny*."

"My mother sings that song, she plays the guitar and leads singing some times." Allyson sang out in her breathy off-key voice. "Lend it, spend it and you'll have so many, they'll roll all over the floor." Her right index finger rolled circles in the air.

"That's good, I've heard that song." Smiled Scott.

"I can't really sing. I don't know why. Everybody in my family plays music and sings. One of the worst things ever in my life was when a drama teacher made me sing "People Who Need People" for a variety show. It was horrible. I don't know why I didn't just say 'no'. I was too shy to say 'no', and then I had to stand alone on stage and try to sing that song."

"I play piano but I really hate recitals," commiserated Scott.

"Well, I do play flute."

"Are you in the band?"

"Yes, I really like the marching band. I even got to lead the parade at a football game this year. I wore a tall fur hat and held a baton. Out in front. It was cool."

"I play drums. I marched last year but not this year. It didn't work into my schedule."

"The funniest thing we did last year," and Allyson became animated with the story of the band at Churchill High School. "We played the opposing team's fight song, only we played it in three-four time, waltz time. It took the fight right out of it. It was so funny."

The two young people scooted their chairs closer together, then they could smell each other's hair, deodorant. He caught a whiff of Allyson's cherry lip gloss.

Allyson laughed her staccato laugh and said, "We can draw the front page of a newspaper with the headline. **Man with Cross on Parade Today at 11:00**."

Scott laid on another kind of joke, "A lightning bolt, hitting the empty cross **Thieves Disappear, Centurions Mystified**." He held his hand in the air showing the imaginary headline.

That evening on the way to vespers Allyson and Scott walked slowly, not holding hands but elbows touching. They were warm in their down-stuffed rain jackets. It is cool in the foothills of the Cascades, even in June. The others walked on up to the wooded chapel. Now everyone knew that something was happening with Allyson and Scott.

That night Allyson and Scott hung out at the young children's playground outside the meeting hall. They perched, talking, on the balance beam, drifted on swings beside each other, played at the slide where Scott caught Allyson as she scooted down into his arms. No kissing on the lips, just hugs, just a touch of her sandy-blond hair, and more and more hugging. They walked side by side, kicking the bark on the packed paths to her cabin.

Inside the girls cabin, Robin, Andrea, and Jane prepared an ambush. *Keep it cool. Wait and watch for Scott to walk away. Ten, nine, eight, seven, six, five—* screech squeal! "Allyson, tell, tell, what happened?" "Did you kiss him?" "What were you doing?" "Do you like him?" "Duh, of course she likes him or she wouldn't have stayed out alone like that."

Every free moment the young lovers met, hiding in among ferns and ancient trees. Every non-free moment they stole away and made lovers' privacy at the far corner of the meeting hall. Without practice or training the two of them fell into the new talent of kissing, kissing with closed eyes, touching cute noses, caressing the long hanging hair of girl and longish hair of boy.

She returned to our small west Eugene house with a terrific glow. In love and torn away from her beloved too soon. He departed going all the way up the Columbia River to The Dalles. It was an impossible distance. I believe that she received three letters and sent I don't know how many. They met once at the Dairy Queen when Scott was at the U. of O. for a conference. For a parent this is the best kind of passion, distance to keep them both safe, but still feeling fire in her body to prove to herself that she was able to love and be beautiful enough to be desired.

__A Poem, Carefree - 1979__
AJB: Remembering Camp Adams 1982
Why analyze the spring
To try to find some hidden meaning
In the season deep?

Only skip outside and leap
Into the joy of brightness
Bask your heart in warmth;
Feel the feelings from the inside out –
    Ecstatic!
    Fanatic!
    Let your mind run free –
    Carefree…

She Received a Love Letter, Christmas 1979

Dear Allyson,

I will be in Springfield Thursday night, and I would like to get together if at all possible. You see my sister and brother-in-law live there and we are going to spend the night, before we head for Arizona.

Do you live very close to Springfield, I hope so. I will call you when I get there and hopefully I could see you later on in the evening.

What kinds of grades did you get last semester, were they pretty good?

I hope you're planning to come up on the 31st still. I wouldn't miss it for the world. I am going to throw a foosball party at my house, but I won't know when it will be. I'll try and let you know as soon as we set a date for it. So you could try to come up for it. We could invite Debbie and Robyn if you like and Andrea too. You could also meet some of my friends.

Whenever you are in The Dalles I wish you would stop by and see me.

I still can't believe I've had a chance to be with such a beautiful girl as you. I've thought about you all the time. You're the only thing on my mind. I wish we could be together always.

Love, Scott

P.S. You'll have to forgive me if I don't write as much as I should. I don't write very good letters. I'll try to send you a post card from Arizona.

P.S.S. I love you!

*   *   *

Friend Coco writes to Allyson,   July 1980,
Allyson's dad's address, 2201 Pecan St., Texarkana, Arkansas.

Hi Allyson!

Sounds like you're having fun. Yes, I'm still terribly jealous about the weather you're having. But the news just was talking about Texas and how the weather is unbearable there, so I think, I change my mind. I'm not that jealous. Wanna hear a miracle? It's sunny here! It's supposed to stay that way.

Your [another summer love interest] Pat sounds so nice. This is how I feel about the problem with Scott; if you're sure you have a hold of your feelings for him then I'd just remember him how he was. If you're not so sure and think you're still in love (infatuation) with him, it might be good for you to see him as he is now, it might totally turn you off. Just remember he's probably getting married and isn't available anymore. Not that it would stop you from trying, but don't forget that point.

About that country club or whatever it is, don't worry about those other girls. Remember you're better or just as good as they are. You're intelligent, cute, and best of all you are yourself, so don't worry and have a ball (oops, that can be dirty.)

You say you're always thinking about Dean well when you find yourself thinking about him, pick up the Bible and start reading it. It may be boring, but it is really good for ya.

Have you gotten your [driver's] license yet? Can you get it if you're from out of state and just visiting?

Ya know I'm just as bad as you are only worse. I dreamed last night I went out with Brent again and had lots of fun, if ya catch my drift. Oh, by the way, did you get my first letter? So you're wondering what I've been doing lately. Well right now I'm just being lazy sitting in the sun. I've been getting in fights with Eric the asshole. I'm on a diet, again. Renee and I are getting to be really good friends again. I just generally am *enjoying the SUNSHINE!*

Nate the kid next door is spazzing out and acting like a dog. What a faggot. Pepe [the dog] says hi.

If you got my first letter what do you think I should do about Jeff? Lisa's going to church and she said that Sunday in church he was holding hands and had his arm around another girl. I don't think he was just flirting. Well, I'll see ya around. Have fun ya'all hear now.

Yere friend Coca-Moe Mow

Chapter Twenty

The Children's Theatre

Beginning in October, 1991 and through the winter of 1992, I produced three original children's plays at the Hult Center in Eugene. I adapted the stories for the stage, directed the actors, designed the scenery, and even constructed half of the costumes. I worked nights and week-ends, never giving myself a moments rest. *Ah hah!* I didn't realize at that time that I was masking my grief and sorrow with frantic activity. This is a form of denial. I was diverting my mind and emotions away from the pain of sorrow.

I agreed to produce, not with marionettes, but with child and adult actors, these three plays: *Robin Hood, No Kissin' and No Killin'; Alice in Wonderland;* and *Hotep the Wonderful Cat of Ancient Egypt.*

At that same time, Bea Garth rented one of my rooms. One January evening, I sat on the floor in my studio with pieces of the Queen of Hearts' costume all around me. I had come to a full stop. I was unable to put needle into cloth. Bea, a professional sculptor, came up to my room.

"I don't know what to do." I wailed. "I can't make a single decision about this costume. I can't go forward, I can't go backward, this is all too much."

Being an experienced fine artist, Bea had faced many crises in getting ready for art shows. "Celeste, trust the process. Just sit in your mess and sooner or later you'll go forward. Hopefully sooner. Don't worry, it'll be all right."

*   *   *

A letter from: *Dorthy Suddath in Seabrook, Texas*
January 3, 1992

Dear Celeste, Today was a beautiful sunny day and the lake was like glass. There was one lone sailboat on the lake and the only sounds were of the sea gulls and an occasional ringing of the sailboats' riggings in our marina. I took this time to go down under our yardarm and offer my prayer for peace [in honor of Allyson's birthday.] I have to admit, I threw a little prayer in there for both of us—for what you have had to endure and for the strength I will need [in my future.] I didn't think Allyson would mind. It was a very special moment. Thank you for letting me share it.—

January 24, 1992--Well, I didn't do a very good job of finishing this letter but my intentions were good. Our lives go on and my husband [Jerry Suddath] shows a strength and goodness that makes me love him even more. He and I have had an incredible relationship, Celeste, and that is what I'm holding on to. His chemo stopped working, so on to a new one, cross our fingers, pray, visualize, hold on to each other and be grateful for this day. He is still working, as he needs to do his academic thing. We hope this new treatment gives us some time. His main concern is that I will be all right. I just feel so lucky for the last 14 years.

At a time like this it sure helps to look at our life together: [Celeste and Dorothy's life together from Junior High on.]: Dad sent me your Robin Hood No Kissin' and No Killin' review [from the newspaper.] "Fun filled and silly; humor and music; fast moving and always inventive; many hits; RAH! RAH! RAH!" That's my Celeste!

I love you lots, Dorothy

*   *   *

Bea brought along her lover to live at our house. He was a suffering poet, a small man with a narrow face. He was afraid of his mother and I, being older and in charge, reminded him of his mother.

I recall the way he crossed a room, not using a straight line through the center, but circuitously and hugging the walls, like a sneaking rat.

When I kicked him out of the shared housing, David Stelle and Bea got together as lovers and caused more drama in the house. That's when David Duemler moved in. He had a Ph.D. in Psychology and was able to figure out how to keep peace in the environment. In fact peace activism was one of his main interests along with, animal rights, and veganism. I became educated to the reality that eating meat was like ingesting violence--the violence toward animals in the meat industry, the crowding of chickens, the restricting of calves, the crippling of dairy animals.

I called David Duemler , Grounded David, and David Stelle, Other David. When Grounded David found me crying he would say, "What's wrong?"

Other David said, "She's crying about Allyson."

Grounded David said, "Oh yes, the Allyson thing," and he would walk on by. He never stopped to cuddle me or speak sweetly. I liked attention, but I also appreciated people who just let me be.

Also in January 1992, I started attending choir practice with my friends Bonny and Yvonne. Central Presbyterian Church was my childhood religious home, and even though I was no longer that kind of Christian, I couldn't stand anymore of the simple music at Unity of the Valley. Also I didn't like the joyous Unity philosophy of "She isn't dead, she's just in transition." *My daughter was dead, damn it, and I wasn't going to be any way happy about it!*

The Presbyterians have such beautiful choir music. I loved singing alto and second soprano. I loved the romantic pieces by Mendelssohn. I felt safe with Yvonne and Bonny and with Bonny's new husband our choir director Paul Guthmuller.

Wednesday afternoons I attended Grief Group, ate supper at the hospital cafeteria and then went to choir practice at 15th and Ferry streets. The harmony, the poetry, the ritual of the Presbyterian Church soothed my soul.

*   *   *

I plowed into *Alice in Wonderland* and hardly saw January, February or half of March. I cast an adult woman to play the part of the Red Queen and at last I began to make progress on the costume. I already had a basic full-skirted dress. I made her some white boxer shorts with red hearts on them. She got to show her underwear several times during the drama when being chased by broccoli or mice. For the dress I decided on an exterior cage design for the Queen, a red padded outside hoop skirt and a tiered padded crown, giving the effect of a chess piece. Her small red-headed ten-year old King of Hearts had a similar red costume. His action was standing beside the queen and taking down notes, rather like a secretary.

I cast four Alices, the part being so big that I decided to divide it among several actresses eight-years old to thirteen: the real-garden-Alice, the expanding-Alice, the talking-to-the-caterpillar-Alice, and the trial-Alice. I brought them on stage all at once for a choreographed dance piece with mirrors and sharp movements. Referring to the *Through the Looking Glass* portion of the story. One of the parents made four matching blue dresses with pinafores.

My daughter Allyson hated *Alice in Wonderland* because it was a play on her name, tauntingly spoken—"Allyson Wonderland." And I never did like *Alice in Wonderland* as a children's show because I think that it is scary, but I was easily persuaded when I was grieving for Allyson. I wickedly dedicated the performance to my dead daughter. She scolded me from the Great Beyond. "Mom, really lame."

I thought of the people who would bring their little children to see this play, which is a series of bad dreams. So I grounded the younger audience members by including oleos, small unrelated scenes, of nursery rhymes: Little Jack Horner, Little Miss Muffet, Little Bo Peep, Old King Cole. For the mock trial, I used the character of the Jack of Hearts who stole the tarts with the Mother Goose characters taking the stand to tell the tale. My favorite musical piece was when the courtroom participants all stood on their chairs to sing *Little Jack Horner*, with the repeated lines "What a good boy, what a good boy, what a good, good, good, good, good boy am I." It was a very operatic finish with a great *tah dah*. This courtroom scene ended with the "Jabberwocky" poem and a giant puppet making his appearance. Alice woke with a start in her garden and her mother (the Red Queen in street clothes) took her into her arms and gave her lots of love and cuddles. This cuddle ending was an acknowledgement of Allyson's and my mother- and- baby rocking game.

My friend Jerry Williams, my professor, and teacher from the University of Oregon drama department, stepped in to help me with the stage settings, which were a complicated system of boxwood hedges. We even used eight of his fancy dining room chairs for the mad tea-party scene.

There was an unprecedented and astounding fifty people in the cast of *Alice in Wonderland*, forty-five who were children and early teens. I was already crazy when I started work on this piece but the job finished me off.

The middle of March, I was exhausted and depressed. I couldn't get out of bed. I played the tapes and music associated with Allyson's death over and over. At church on the night of Good Friday I wore a gray hat with my black veil over it. From the bell choir, Bonny rang the largest handbell thirty-five times, the years of Jesus's life, the candles of the church went out and we were left in darkness. Yvonne hung on to me, while in the darkness, in my mind I counted to the year 27, Allyson's age when she died. Yvonne has a daughter and understood the pain and joy of that relationship.

I was smart enough to know that eventually I had to get out of bed. There was yet one more children's play to produce.

Baby steps:

First day: *Put your foot on the floor. Sit up. Walk down stairs.*
Second day: *Open front door, walk across porch.*
Third day: *Walk on sidewalk to edge of property.*
Fourth day: *Drive car to gym, listen to the radio, drive home.*
Fifth day: *Go inside gym, suit-up in exercise clothes and do stretches.*
Sixth day: *Do some weight-lifting.*

It was the weight-lifting that got me in trouble. I was working on the lat pull- down machine and putting the bar behind my neck. Pull, pull, pull. I felt like screaming. OK. I stopped and walked to the other part of the weight room, no one was here. I looked out at the pool. Everyone was in the water swimming.

I returned to the lat pull-down machine. My insides felt swirly. I decided to scream. Opening my chest, my heart, I pulled down against the resistance. And I yelled. "A-L-L-Y-S-O-N!!" All was quiet, then I heard the sound of a window sliding open above me. A head peered down at me from the rafters. (It turns out that there is an office up there over the weight room.)

"Are you all right, lady?"

"Excuse me, I thought I was alone, you know, I was working out kind of loudly, sorry."

"OK," said the mysterious stranger. But in the next instance a young woman lifeguard rushed in.

"Are you OK? Someone said there's something wrong in here. Are you all right?"

"I'm fine. I just, you know, was working out and groaned and pulled on the weights and made some noise."

"Come with me into the dressing room. Is this your sweatshirt?"

"Yes, that's my purple sweatshirt."

"Come with me, won't you?"

I followed her across the pool deck and into the women's locker room. Jan, my friend from choir, saw us go by and came out of the pool. Dripping, she followed us. I had begun to cry and shake.

Jan spoke to the youthful guard. "It's fine, I got it. I'm a friend of hers. Really, she's totally all right." The guard left and hurried back to her duties and Jan sat with me as I explained what had happened.

Chapter Twenty-One

Letters, Journals, Mills College
Library and Beyond

Her friend from Mills College wrote me a letter.

Dear Celeste,   Chicago, Il. February 24, 1992

Talking to several of Allyson's friends,… we've concluded that each should remember Allyson in her own, individual way. Perhaps this is the most appropriate because like all good friends, Allyson meant different things to different people. Also I must admit that we are all still having a difficult time accepting our loss.

What I've decided to do, and this will help me acknowledge my loss and to remember Allyson for the rest of my life, is to make a yearly donation to Mills in her memory. Allyson is as much a part of Mills to me as the place itself and I want to keep both in my thoughts and heart forever. It was because of Mills that Allyson and I became friends, and this gift is one that I truly want to give.

I know Allyson loved cats, and if you do too, you'll be happy to know that my husband and I recently adopted two lynx-point Siamese kittens, a brother and sister we named Samson and Sheba. They are now 10 weeks old and as I was just writing this sentence, Sheba leapt off her cat scratcher and on to my shoulder, so you can see they are very active!! I hope all is well with you, Celeste, please know that we all still care for Allyson so much and will always miss her.

Love, Liz Bloomer,

*   *   *

AJB   **Mills College,**   **Journal 1983**

Books and more books, I'll never be able to bear the smell of a library again. Dusty, musty and stale is the smell that gives me perpetual headaches. My eyes feel heavy and my body's tired, but I must smile and be of service to the whims of the entire campus.

Ah, but the sweet smell of money, and as long as there is no shelving to do, I can survive. Or I can target books, or cut up paper or some other mindless task that allows my mind to be anywhere but here.

On a river rafting, or in the ocean sailing, or in Eugene soaking up the rain. Or I can dream of a really exciting job as a movie maker or movie actress or clinical psychologist or bartender, or anything but shelving books and stamping books or organizing endless pamphlets and reserves or listening to a half crazy supervisor telling me I have to check my roommate's I.D. to make sure she really goes here.

The only thing I'll really miss are the ghosts in the basement and on the back stairs, but I'll see them again when I return to make my film on the gradual psychological deterioration of a library loan desk assistant who sinks deeper into insanity every time she shelves books among the ghosts of the basement.

Until then...

*   *   *

April 20/21, 1992 was the first anniversary of her death. I had another dramatic ceremony, this time down at the Willamette River. I hired a bag-piper to stand on the bank and play. My brother, Winston, attended and a young woman played the flute. I made candleholder boats and floated them.

*   *   *

I remembered from authentic movement class that when a person is discharging emotion it helps to have a witness. A sort of

"Mommy, watch me. Mommy, look at me. Look at me, watch me Mommy," kind of scene, so I called a member of the Grief Group and asked her to come to my house.

I had a stack of papers to take care of. I was supposed to file Allyson's taxes for 1990 and part of '91. I had half of her files, (Allyson's Dad, Lawton Bennett, had the other half.) I decided to work with Naomi in the back yard, showing her what I thought of taxes and paper work.

I sat Naomi in a lawn chair. The patio table was full of old catalogues and useless pieces of paper. "I just want you to watch and understand my frustration with the paper work left over from Allyson's death."

She nodded her head, keeping her mouth shut.

My discussion of the paperwork started simply enough and then accelerated into a tantrum of giant proportions: "Papers, papers, all I have left of my daughter is a stack of papers. This is what I think of the papers." *Rip, rip, stomp, stomp.* "Cut me some slack! What kind of idiots would have dead people paying taxes? I can't believe what they're asking me to do. Fill out tax forms?" *Tear, tear, throw, throw.* "Do papers breathe? Do tax forms hug or kiss? Do you understand? I long for the touch of my Allyson; I long to hear her laugh; to talk to her on the phone. All I have left is this ridiculous pile of paper." Repeatedly I picked up papers and threw them violently down, picking up and tossing. "Give me my daughter back. I want her to come home to me. My arms are empty, my heart is broken. I can't stand life without her…"

I looked at Naomi, she nodded, she wept, and she did not say a word. Her attitude encouraged me. *Go on, Celeste, do it, Celeste.*

If we had been in the southern black Baptist Church, she and others in the congregation would have shouted, "Amen, sister. Tell it, sister. Lord help Celeste, she is suffering. Amen. Hallelujah, give her comfort, Lord. Take her into your embrace and give her comfort, Lord. Listen to her sorrows for your shoulders are broad, Lord, you can share her burdens, give comfort to this wounded mother. Amen. Amen. Hallelujah."

*   *   *

A letter to myself:

Dear Celeste, I am proud of you. As the Beatles song says, you have indeed taken 'a sad thing to make it better.' You listened to your heart and followed your intuition. You listened to others when things were not *your* way and accepted the changes and the happenings.

You honored your feelings whenever they happened and tried to act authentically even if it hurt or even if it was embarrassing. You are truly a brave lady with very strong character. As I used to quote from *Grooks,* the poetry book by Piet Heine, "If it doesn't kill you outright, it makes you stronger." Now just be gentle and slow with yourself. One day at a time, one task at a time, and we will continue to get better and better.

Love, Celeste Rose.

"Wow, what a woman!"

Chapter Twenty-Two

Weaving a Cloak of Recovery

There's the colorful opera coat that Allyson gave me when she was too poor to pay her rent, there's her pinkie-ring on my finger that catches the light, there's seeing a young woman with henna hair disappearing around the corner.

We had a family too and the family is also gone into the past. There's the love poem that my husband wrote to me, the carving that he made that sits on my kitchen window, there is the photograph of my son when he was a child and eager to live each day, there are the glass jars filled with plum jelly catching the sun from an August day. There is the memory of the deep furry coat of the sheltie dog and there is the crazed calico cat. There is always the music, the songs and the instruments.

Weave and spin, weave and spin.

There's the counting of the days: the date she died, the day she was born. These days are not marked on the calendar but are remembered. There are days that especially catch my heart and the moments when the mourners cried together, holding each other, receiving comfort. Her blanket and her bear are still with me. But her dresses, her art work, her baby clothes have been given away.

Then the recovery days arrived: I forgot her birthday, her death day became just another date. I now enjoy the sunset without feeling pain in my heart.

Spin and weave, spin and weave, constructing a cloak of recovery, a garment first worn and touched, with wind blowing the sleeves, as I stood in a dramatic pose on the top of a little hill. That sacred garment now hangs in the closet, gathering a row of dust where the clothes hanger supports the shoulders.

Oh, that old thing. I remember how hard I worked to weave and spin, to build that costume to follow death and learn to dance. I danced a dance for the two of us. Weave and spin, weave and spin. On the grassy knoll, elbows bent, hands to the sky and feet tracing a circle round, I am the woman who learned to walk again when all was lost, who chanced upon an inner song to dance, who dances now with life. I follow the sunshine and trace the path of the wind, I sing all the songs I ever knew, and you'll see me disappear over the hill where everything is new.

Eugene, February 14, 2012

I saw their car parked in my driveway, opened the front door and brought my armful of groceries in the door and set them on the piano bench. The washing machine was chugging away, Mike Droske was working on his laptop at the dining room table, thirty-one-year-old Holly Mae Bennett, also known as my granddaughter, also known as Mrs. Mike Droske, also known as Doctor of Veterinary Science, stood folding clothes on the other side of the table.

"Hi, Grandma, surprise! We just thought we'd come down to Eugene and see you… and do our laundry." She laughed.

"What a domestic scene! Glad to see you darlings." I gave her a hug. She smelled like warm dryer-cleaned clothes. "Are you staying overnight?"

"Yes, but we'll be out late. Tonight we're going to go to Jason's and play some music. Tomorrow we can have breakfast with you and have a chance to catch up."

My heart felt warm, like sunshine happiness in the dreary Oregon afternoon.

Holly and her husband live in Portland, she works as a Veterinarian at an animal ER clinic.

She is so like a daughter to me.

Is it said, or shall I say it?

The Beginning

She led me to the floor,
An invitation to dance.
For life, there is more,

...A Second Chance.

Appendix One
Stories, Journals, Poems and Letters

Eugene with Celeste

I am feeling healthy now at the age of 73. The date is April 21, 2012, that is twenty-one years since Allyson's death. I am happy with my life. I have just reopened a package sent long ago from my ex-husband. There are more of Allyson's journals, poems, and letters in here: as a Mills College graduate, in San Francisco with no jobs and shared housing, with details of the exotic dancing and some childhood ramblings including a child's short story. There are frightening experiences that she kept from me. At the time, she preferred to tell me that all was well and that she was comfortable and successful.

The code names at Mills College for herself and Pamela were: Allyson as Inertia Rhapsody and Pamela as Ruby Tuesday.

Allyson Journals – The Dark Side

AJB: Place: Café Flora,   3/15/88

I used to live off the streets, I didn't live on the streets now, but I was so busy paying rent I couldn't eat. I was getting slammed against the wall by the snake – lease holder—slammed of all my cash for a pink room with no sunlight and an empty refrigerator.

So I'd hang out at my "fave" café, my friends giving me coffee for almost nothing--all that coffee and I wouldn't notice I was hungry-- and I'd buy huge bags of potatoes… Cheap food was fine, rice, potatoes, noodles, but by itself I wouldn't eat it. Lost 15 pounds. So I started shoplifting, not much, just butter and gourmet salad dressing, anything to make my food taste good. I didn't feel bad about it either and I never got caught. When it's survival, not getting caught is the law. I found some bagels at the corner of Haight and Masonic once, a huge bag of them. I think that they must have been left out by the Holy Bagel for the street people. I took four of them and they got me through a week.

Every night I went to the café and talked to Lisa. She'd give me soup sometimes if the boss wasn't around. I made a lot of friends there. Later I'd go up to Nightbreak in the upper Haight. It was a place to listen to music, some really warped kind of bands, like

"Standing Naked," "Miss Kitty and the Psyco Souls," or "Radical Puppy." I'd hang out there, smoke, look bored, and go home at 2:00 am. I found some great things on the street at that hour—once a big black overcoat and another time, in front of the St. Vincent de Paul, I found a half dozen light green tea cups.

Going to work at 9 a.m. every day wasn't easy on this schedule, but there was too much crazy dealings happening at home to hang there. Plus, I hate the color pink. I went mad in that room.

One day when I was new in the neighborhood, I went to the corner deli, I was in line for a cup of coffee, and this guy with nothing in his eyes was being strange. He left and a woman in line and I exchanged a look. We both had seen the nothingness in his eyes and with this bond we sat and had our coffee together. She was wearing dark glasses. She started talking and talking. She was sad. And angry. She told me that she'd just torn up all her art. She took off her dark glasses, showing me her eyes that were swollen and black. "I've been in a fight with my boyfriend. He's a musical genius. Maybe you've seen him at the Haight Street Fair."

She and I became friends. I needed one. We both were living on nothing. At this time she was worse off than me. I invited her to my house for French toast. She was one of the people I went to Nightbreak with sometimes. When I had nothing, she fed me, tomato and parsley sandwiches.

Once when we were walking about she had 2 bucks and I had nothing. She gave me one. She said "You should have enough for at least a cup of coffee." Great woman. Too bad she hung out with a guy who beat her blind. Too bad she did so much speed and heroin. Worked in daycare, when she worked, she was great with children. I don't know where she is now. Rumor is she went to a shelter and dried out. I hope that's true.

All my friends did drugs. No junkies though. But they were all cool with me being straight.

One thing about being on the street, you always have friends, but no real friends. I didn't have a best friend for a long time. My friends worked in the cafés. Convenient. I always knew where to find them. The café was my living room. I needed a buddy though.

Always alone. Not quite part of the scene I was in. It was objective, watching it go by like a film. But the hunger wasn't objective. I almost picked up a piece of chocolate off the street once. I was craving it so badly. But Linda, from Eugene, gave me a brownie at the café. I was so grateful that when I won tickets to UB40 I took her. UB40 is a British reggae/pop band. I was very lucky then. Never went to a show I had to pay for. Made friends so I was on guest lists everywhere. And I listened to the radio and won tix to shows, movies, So I took Linda to UB40 weird show in Berkeley. I'd been walking the streets of SF all summer.

Berkeley, in contrast, was so white, so preppie. The show was thronging with young rich kids from the Berkeley hills. Before, when I went to Mills College, street people in Berkeley seemed so out-of-control crazy but now it's all so tame, so clean, so white.

I wore a hole through my boots that summer. I could feel the street as I walked. I sensed the street as I slept. Then the slamming-snake gave me notice. Gave me motivation to leave, twenty days notice, motivation. I had a dream. I dreamed I woke up inside my sleeping bag warm and cozy. I put my head out. And I was on the street corner with street people around, messing with me. I felt trapped and vulnerable. That's all I remember. I didn't end up on the street. But ... That's a different story.

Stream of Consciousness

AJB: When you're on the street, that's life. It's tunnel vision. Survival, existence. You walk the soles out of your shoes so you feel the street with every step and will take food whenever it's offered or better yet speed. It keeps you going, and you don't need to eat. You just need the cash for your cigarettes. You can find clothes on the corner. You can get drugs from your friends for a while, while they're still friends. Get some cash, somehow. Need that speed. Yeah man, I'd love to hear you play. Can you put me on the list? No problem. I know the doorman. Man I need a place to stay, she's cute. So you like the band. Yeah the bass player's a friend of mine put me on the list...continuous bullshit need a place to stay, dancing in the Street.

I was walking down Church Street the other day and saw an old drunk beating off in an alley. That was sad, to care so little, just need to get off.

Just outside the door – the Latino boys are so proud of their cocks.

They want to share it with the world.

"Hey baby, want a vanilla milkshake?"

"Fxxx off and die."

"You have beautiful round eyes."

"You are very cute."

"Don't be scared of me."

"When I saw you getting off the train, I was struck by your beauty."

"I have to introduce myself. My name is Leonard."

"Hi Leonard. Bye Leonard."

"Oh, OK Sorry. *Ciao*."

Lame pick up…I love the city.

I love the Mission.

I love the smell of piss.

From Inertia Rhapsody,

I need you Ruby Tuesday,

 Ruby I'm sorry I haven't written.

Where are you now?

France; or maybe Colorado

Inertia is inert these days but looking for the

 Outside force to get her going again.

Ruby. I wish you were here in the Mission hole.

This little world of rotting fish

Mixed with a little urine on the street.

Piss Alley.

Mills College

AJB: She cried uncontrollably in the midst of her chaotic dorm room with the dirty white rug that she hadn't bothered to vacuum for months. Made up one layer of the floor. The second, a layer of clothes and books and papers which she flung about each morning in search of something to wear and work that must be done. The hangers in her closet were empty with the exception of a few dresses that she never touched.

Finally exhausted from her sobbing, she walked outside into the unreal campus which denied the reality of the urban world outside the fence surround the little world of Eucalyptus trees. A haven for squirrels, birds and women with academia on the brain. She walked along the most deserted most dangerous paths of campus until she reached the remote grave of the founder of the prestigious community. She sat and smoked her Camel Lights thrown the cigarette butts onto the grave of their founder as if they were roses.

AJB: a game. It's only a game. It's only a game. It's only a game. It's only a game.
It's only a game. It's only a game. It's only a game. It's only a game. It's only a game.
It's only a game. It's only a game. It's only a game. It's only a game. It's only a game.
It's only a game. It's only a game. It's only a game. It's only a game. It's only a game. It's only a game. It's only a game. It's only a game. It's only a game. It's only a game. It's only a game. It's only a game. It's only a game. It's only a game. It's only a game. It's only a game. It's only a game. It's only a game. It's only a game. It's only a game. It's only a game. It's only a game. It's only a game. It's only a game. It's only a game. It's only a game. It's only a game. It's only a game. It's only a game. It's only a game. It's only a game. It's only a game. It's only a game. It's only a game. It's only a game. It's only a game. It's only a game. It's only a game. It's only a game. It's only a game. It's only a game. It's only a game. It's only a game. It's only a game. It's only a game. It's only a game. It's only a game. It's

July 12, 1991
From: Pamela Rhodes (Ruby Tuesday)
To: Celeste Rose

Thank you for your letter concerning Allyson. I am so sorry. It's been very hard for me since I received your letter. I spent the most time of anyone with Allyson her last year at Mills. Her death hit me very hard. I agree that It was her death and she left us early for her own reasons. I also believe as you do that she was very strong spiritually and she is happy, free and at peace, however I find myself sitting in front of a very big hole in my life that was my friendship with Allyson. She was a wonderful friend always.

She possessed a combination of wisdom, openness and great sense of humor – it was much needed some nights late in the computer center. My code name was Ruby Tuesday and her code name on the computer was Inertia Rhapsody. I kept a copy of all our little computer messages that we sent back and forth that year. She always left me some message that made me laugh and realize exams or whatever wasn't as bad as it seemed. One time when things were particularly bad, she took the time to write me a whole page message that only had one phrase: It's only a game.

This type of "Crazy Wisdom" made me laugh so hard and put things in perspective.

I've been procrastinating terribly on this letter. Some part of me feels that if I write this letter what happened will be real, and if I don't she's going to be calling me on the phone. Or, I'll be able to see her when I'm in San Francisco. We had plans to get together this summer. Every time I was in the Bay Area, we didn't get to see each other. She had her job and her classes. I was so happy for her that she was busy and productive and happy. Though we did talk on the phone. Every time I was there, I'm so sad I didn't get to see her.

If you ever feel the desire to talk about Allyson I hope you would feel free to call me. Allyson was a great listener, and I hope that I can offer you that kind of support that she frequently gave me.

Love Pamela.

Poet unknown

Dear Allyson,
Your death stopped my heartbeat and then it went on.
Your absence made the silence deafening.
Your pace, or rather, none of it, failed
To click-cadence or interrupt ours
And your spirit soaring, tipped the earth's scale.

At first I think: Which of us is diminished;
We, by our loss of you, or you, by your journey?
Yet, aren't we enriched and energized
                    by our appreciation of time?
Are we? And aren't we touched by all of
The scripts you wrote and acted in?   Brava!

Tu amici

*   *   *

AJB SF: Once I lived in a place that was so cold, I couldn't
stand to be there. The room-mates were cold too. My café habit
became increasingly neurotic. After work, Ground Zero until closing,
house coffee. After closing I went to Café Flora until closing for
espresso con panne. To Orphan Andy's for bad coffee to calm down.
Orphan Andy's never closed so I stayed there until I was so
exhausted, I was about to drop. My room was so cold and dark I was
late to work more and more. I couldn't get out of bed and there was
no light to signal morning. Almost got fired. I started chain smoking
during the café scene. I got sick when I went home for Christmas.
Very sick, tonsillitis. But I was home and it was such a relief to have
someone to take care of me. Not to have to worry about work. It was
only worse when I came back. I knew then I needed to change things.
So did my boss. I was put on probation, and requested a cut in hours

to look for a second job. About the time I found my second job I met Larry. And that's how I left the Haight for the Mission. One hole for another. But Larry's my best friend as well as my lover.

I just moved somewhere very weird, but I took it because I sensed two of the roommates were very cool and the room gets tons of light. And Larry is helping me make my room into my space.

Mr. Wong and the Filipino couple put no energy into the household and created plenty of mess. Mr. Wong with his bad aim at the toilet and the Filipino couple with their fried foods in the kitchen and their neglect in cleaning up after themselves. The stove is covered with grease. But some very positive energy is coming out of my energy in cleaning up a bit. I agree that we shouldn't clean up after the others all the time, but I think with joined forces we could create a better living environment. We'll see.

8/12:   I'm in the neurology clinic. My horoscope today says a health problem is psychological. Maybe I should see a psychologist instead of a neurologist.

I'm so tired of it all. There's so much stuff to deal with. I want to quit my job, but now would be the worst possible time for my boss. It would kill him, and it would be awful for my job record. I'm terminally responsible. In this case that could be true.

This job is not conducive to writing movies.

*   *   *

Steve is back in town and I am returning to café. I'm thinking if I put the creative environment of the past together with current motivational forces (the *Gohonzon*) I'll be able to begin producing again and maybe completing work – a first. I'll start my ideas in the cafés and continue turning my room into a good work environment to do the hard core work.

"We all have phases of manipulation." Steve and I used to come here to write. I used to come here to eavesdrop. I met the first man I ever made love to here. I met Peter the word man here. I used to come here with Andrea and David for brunch. I used to come here and write love letters to Paul. Maybe if I go to the old places my imagination will return. And maybe I'll find Steve.

Today I'll just write and maybe something will come. I'm thinking I like the idea of joy and beauty in things shattered. Terror in the clean immaculate retail world. I'm thinking that I like the idea of not knowing the line of reality. In general for a movie. Specifically still and moving lines of silence, perhaps silence. In silence is a deafening sound where each creak or little noise is a distraction. And yet in the noise of a busy café is the silence I need to write. I'm thinking. Where shall I start with " Z?" The wild frantic eyes searching for a friend in the woman who sells her truffles? Steve would say, if he came in, "You're still here? But what's this you're drinking, tea!" Yeah, it's been months since I've done this scene. Larry sucked me in beyond control but I'm back finding my words again.

Silence.

There's Rachel Reilly of Mills. She doesn't see me. She was into film. I wonder what she is doing? I like ceiling fans, visually-- ceiling fans and Botticelli prints.

There is an immense intuition that works within my life. Rachel there with her cigarette talking. I feel like I'm back in the Mills Grill watching MASH.

I'm in a dream. But if I continue writing them down I can keep the flow of thoughts while bringing a concrete workable reality to the art inside me. I must keep writing if I am to get anywhere, if any dream of a movie is to be made concrete. Keep going like the ceiling fan. Silence – a ceiling for unmoving.

Just talked to Rachel. She might buy my super – 8 splicer/editing system. Would help pay for the equipment I need!

Present the unreal as the real.

I look to you for inspiration, a muse for this static mind.

Today I find joy and beauty in things shattered, a broken mirror, another street find. There's another pretty boy with one curly lock fallen in his face, dressed in black tuxedo-ware.

Jet set of San Francisco, the new trend is serial monogamy. 1) An AIDs test every 6 months. 2) Condoms and lubricating gel. 3)

Drug users increasingly selfish with their personalized needles and bleach bottle.

Café's for the rich and famous with gourmet chocolate, gourmet ice-cream, and the gourmet coffee like what I sell. I work for Clyde in the Mission District. Selling cups of coffee or bags of special grinds. Smiling always smiling even when I'm dying to escape on my trip to Jamaica. Tower records is bound to draw my name for the trip to Jamaica. I need a big benefit so I can give a real convincing experience. Yeah Baby. Praise Buddha-hood. I need more than anything to take a break. I dream of summer in Eugene, sunbathing topless next to the rapids of the McKenzie River. Rafters only able to catch a fleeting glimpse of my breasts before the rapids takes them away.

Leaping off bridges into swimming holes, going under, and feeling that fleeting sense of no control while I sink and fight my way to the surface – wholly immersed in the cool river water. Washed clean of the stench of the Mission District with rotting vegetables, rotting urine and feces, and bums asking always for more spare change.

On the corner, Hispanic evangelists screaming in Spanish, which I don't understand, and sometimes, on a good day, the old black man playing his blues guitar on the same corner. Playing the sound that takes me back to the beautiful part of the old cotton fields back home. The porches where the common folk sit to cool off while the whites keep cool in their multitude of artificial environments. My life is a never ending layer of experiences.

AJB: Spiritual: Letter to Niike, How to gain in daily life. Correct attitude of faith till the last moment. What does lotus sutra mean? The law of *Nam-Myoho renge-kyo*, the 3 great secret laws, the *Gohonzon*, highest Buddhist teaching of a particular age – the Latter Day of the Law. Intent of Lotus Sutra – all people have the Buddha in them – so we must do *Shakaboku* and we must treat everyone equally.

Nam-Myho-Renge-Kyo is a phrase with many layers of meaning which we begin to understand and perceive more and more as we practice. But to skim the surface:

Nam is an nonorific prefix meaning devotion to
Myoho Renge Kyo is the title of the Lotus Sutra in Japanese.
Myoho = mystic law
Renge = cause and effect
Kyo = sound and vibration.
Surface definition. Devotion to the mystic law
      of cause and effect through sound vibration.

Budget: Rent $375,
Utilities $25,
Transportation $30,
Food $200,
Buddhist Supplies $30.
Entertainment $30.
    Total = $690

AJB: **A Poem**
I fell asleep within your arms but
When I woke I was alone.
I long for dreams
I can live --
Longingness.
Prefabricated dreams, a hope.

I am never alone
When I sleep with my mind but then wake into coldness –
The floor is cold.
Jumpingness.

The turtles are endangered of being blown away
You cry inside me – You are my people,
Me being hurt, please, let me destroy myself.

My name is Allyson Bennett and I've been practicing this
Buddhism for 1 yr 5 months. I want to be a film maker. Its been a
dream for years and although I did a lot of talking about it I honestly

didn't have any clue as to the 1st step to take to move me towards that goal. I got to feeling paralyzed and inadequate, if full of hot air no action.

I'd resisted chanting for a good 10 months since my first meeting, but I finally decided it couldn't hurt, and if it helped great. I'd test it experimentally.

On the top of my list of *determints* for 1988. Get a job in the film industry.

I was constantly restricted time wise and financially by my work situation, I hardly used my new camera which made me feel like an idiot. How devoted could I be if I couldn't even use the benefit I had. I quit my job and began a 6 month partial employment spree moving from one part-time and temp job to another.

In December I answered a small ad in the Chronicle. Small Production Company, ad asst. under qualified as I was I put my all into applying. I hadn't worked so hard for a job ever before. It really reinforced in me what I wanted to do. I chanted for them to choose the right person. I gained tremendous respect for them and they like me too. I was #2 out of 40 applicants.

Omega. I finally took a part time job at a lab, a job I knew would be a drag but it was related to film. The invoices I filed had the names of production companies on them and I took calls from people at companies. I did my best to learn what I could about the industry while I was there, and in the meantime charted with the REEL DIRECTORY in front of me.

I then got another Part time office job for an underwater construction company. The owner turned out to be a client of the lab I worked at, he does underwater videos.

I started sitting in on a film class at the STAT I signed up for workshops and to volunteer in the studio of Channel 25 which turned out to be a few blocks from my house.

Then at work one day I ran into one of the partners from Omega. He said they needed interns. (Interns meaning college students who can work for free.) I called him later to discuss it. I told him I couldn't afford to work for free and gave him a minimum subsistence rate.

If he accepted this I would have to rearrange my schedule at my other office job which was still just 2 weeks old. So basically I was trying to arrange a salary and get 2 different employers to accept schedules that still fulfilled the others needs.

I also needed to survive financially. That Saturday I chanted 6 hours, on Sunday I went to YWD activities. I had already gotten Joe to agree to a minimum wage. And gotten Tom to agree to a schedule. But this schedule would require Joe to make certain concessions schedule wise. I was so scared. Things were changing so fast I was doing so much. I felt if he accepted my schedule. I gave 2 weeks notice the next day at the Lab and have fit in what I can each week at Omega. I've been working 3 jobs then the last 2 weeks.

I am so happy I was able to make this all happen through chanting. *Nam –Myoho-Ringe – Kyo.*

All it would've taken for me to go off track would have been to get scared, put on the breaks, stop chanting. I was scared, fear of success is very real, but I was able to break through that barrier and get my first job at a production company.

John's Café – between 23rd and 24th – good breakfast.
1st week of August
Dream: (First night sleeping in new flat with mice.) I was in the Bartlett flat walking down hall and ran into a very large mouse. We both wanted the other to go away. Expected to scare the other off – so it was a stand off. We both became hysterical, the mouse began running in circles, I picked it up by the tail and bashed it into the wall. It twisted and bit me, but barely broke the skin. I bashed it into the wall until it went limp.

I told dream to a customer at Clyde's Coffee Shop. (Cindie) . She said perhaps there's someone I want to bash into a wall. I told it to flat manager Terry and he said that perhaps I don't need to get that violent, but it sounds like I'm repressing some anger. I agree. While writing to Paul I became very angry when I described my job to him. (I feel as though I'm sucking Clyde's cock for a living – metaphorically speaking).   Anyway it's 9:35 at Café Nidal and I guess I better get going to another day of oral stimulation.

Lusty lady

AJB: <u>Feb. 17, 1989</u>

Totally completely broke, in the world of hunger and catering to that world in return. So I've made the move to my first "alternative" job, i.e. not a straight job. Last Friday I auditioned at the Lusty Lady to be an erotic dancer. It started as an experiment. I think, I'll just go down and check the place out, and fill out an application. I think, I'll call for an audition. Might as well try it. Everyone there is really friendly and nice. I've felt comfortable from the start…whereas other jobs I've applied for, at the law firms etc, straight jobs, people are so insincere, creepy. I'd rather work at the Lusty Lady where there is no pretense. I'm sure they have their own games, but the financial district scene really nauseates me.

There's something very strange about showing my private parts to strangers all day. It doesn't bother me, but I do worry about getting a good show together, being really erotic, exotic, and gracious. In my own personal life, I'm used to being straight forward—never learned to be a tease—never learned the womanly games and talk which would come in handy now. I really don't know what to say.

The audition was really exciting, sitting in the office talking and talking, putting it off. (Take off my clothes and go out there and then do what? Not a clue what to do.) But I did it. And I watched myself do it in the mirrors around the stage. I saw myself naked dancing in my Grandma's heels with the rhinestones up the arch. I was shaking, adrenaline pumping through, breasts shimmying, hips grinding, or trying to. Awkward, as I was scared out of my mind.

So Tuesday, Valentines Day was my first day. I just wore my Grandma's heels and black net gloves that I borrowed from Kingman. I took the gloves off when I discovered they were bleeding black everywhere. The heels came off when I found walking difficult. I became amazingly tired after a couple of hours and found myself better able to dance in bare feet. Six hours I danced. Six hours of touching myself, showing my breasts, being flirtatious and flashing the more intimate parts of my body.

The gentlemen customers sat in individual glassed-in booths around the dance floor. The business men threw coins, quarters, at the glass making popping sounds, to show their appreciation.

How did it make me feel? A day of bumping and grinding? Lonely. All day my body was bare to strangers, so I think I kept my heart concealed, especially since I don't know the other women there yet, and all I could see and feel upon closing my eyes was me curled up with Scott. Oh No! Not another Scott! My journals have too much experience with that name. At least he's not a drummer. OK, who's this Scott dude. He's blond, he's a socialist, but he doesn't expect me to be one. He's a smiling socialist, not a screaming one.

Anyway, Monday I called Scott because I thought maybe he had called me, for a second, actually, I knew it was an old message on my machine, but I felt like talking so I called him as the message confusion provided a great excuse. We talked an hour or more, and then he said, "Let's go to the beach."

Beaches make me uncomfortable, beaches are romantic. I don't know yet what he wants. I don't know yet what I want, but inside I wanted company. I want a friend. I know that. So, sure let's go to the beach. At the beach he showed me how amazing the moon is at that angle at that time of night. Half moon on the waves. And I talked incessantly rambling on and on about everything from childhood to virginity, to stories to everything because rambling is what I do when I feel romance in the air and I'm uncomfortable because I'm not sure how I feel. He'd take a step towards me as we stood talking, I'd become more animated and I stepped away. What an idiot. So finally after several hours of this he took me home. He probably thinks –oh it doesn't matter if he has a heart he can deal, if his heart's in his pants then he might think I'm silly and lose interest.

I'm not even looking, so why should I worry. But he did kiss me goodnight. It was like a first kiss, awkward and searching and wandering and wondering. Is it real? Or is it Memorex. It was enough of a kiss to make me wish that the arms I was in on Tuesday night were his.

But I learned a lot.   I went to a Buddhist meeting, a *Shakabuku* meeting at Janet's and I had the privilege of doing *Geshu* with Noriyo.   And we got a guest. He spoke no English but by showing him the Spanish pamphlet we were able to interest him.   All the guests ended up being Spanish so Rudy and Vivienne ran the meeting.   George, our *geshu*, received *Gohanzon* Wednesday! And when I went home Tuesday I wasn't depressed anymore.   I can be happy alone, because I'm not alone. I've got an enormous support network.   But I blew it Wednesday and Thursday.   My *Gongyo* and *Daimaku* has been barely there, or not there.   And I've retracted to my glazed eye stare doing nothing feeling sad.   And I know if I'd just move, if I'd just do *Gongyo* then I could get a lot done, I could accomplish things, but for some weird reason I fall into that.   Without *Gohanzon* I'd sit and stare the rest of my life.

Sometimes my dreams overwhelm me.   Why can't I just do it. Every step is so hard.   I just want to be a filmmaker but I don't know where to start, what to do, have to organize my life.   I'm closer and closer though.   I can feel it, and can only attribute it to chanting.   It's the only thing I've changed.

> Poem
> Body and soul
> The big black hole
> Would eat me up
> Into eyes
> Glazed.
> A stare – I could stare
> At a wall or a heater curled up
> Afraid to move – I'd get cold
> Not doing anything. Just a Stare.

AJB: **An Experience**
Before I started chanting I had lots of ideas about what I wanted to do. I want to be a filmmaker. No I don't want to go to

school. I can't deal with school. No I don't want to go to LA. I can't deal with LA. I can't get a job in the industry because I don't have any experience. All day I talked about what I wanted to do, I talked a lot. And then when I went home I would go in my room and close the door and stare at the wall. I could stare for hours, afraid to move. There was a big black hole inside me that engulfed me and my eyes would glaze over and I would stare and dream about all the things I would do and people I would meet. People who knew me wouldn't sense this part of me, no one knew but me, that I couldn't get anything done. Sometimes the black hole would get out of control and I'd get really depressed and cry. I don't know what to do. Well what do you want to do? I want to be a filmmaker, I want to paint etc. etc. And my then boyfriend, Larry, helped arrange my room and fix things so I could do my art, so I could write, so I'd have space but then I'd still stare.

When I received *Gohonzon,* I saw the darkness, and struggled to practice consistently, but it was hard to battle the darkness. I perfected the *Gohonzo*n quickly and had a few benefits, but I still felt lost and unable to chant every day. After two months I knew I'd never know how the practice worked if I didn't practice consistently so in the February *Shakabuku* campaign, I determined to go to every meeting possible and chant to understand *Shakabuku*. During this campaign Larry gave me a 16mm Bolex Camera. I *Shakabukued* one person, and I remember my life at that time as changing from dark to light.

Lines from the exotic dancer to the gentlemen clients.

"Gee, " clueless, "What does that mean?"

"You don't get to see that until you look into my eyes."

"I'm a virgin, actually we're all virgins and it's a prerequisite to working here."

Who are these ladies at the *Lusty Lady*? Jody is tall, chocolate dark, and lithe and perky. She wears a black silk robe. She is beautiful. Her boyfriend came to see her Tuesday and that really made her mad. There is no love at the *Lusty Lady*. It's all just physical stimulation for one purpose only. There is no pretense of love, so I guess when your boyfriend shows it must hurt inside.

A woman named Trashy gives that cold exterior. She doesn't give a damn. "What's your name , Trashy?"

"Trashy Bitch, Ms. Bitch to you."

She's tough. She was tough at the meeting too. She disagreed with the idea to have a man employed for the assistant show director. She's nice though but I've yet to see her heart.

February 18,

Today is going to be really rough. It's the Chinese New Year Parade. That means lots of people, the streets packed, Kearny St. so full of people. Lots of customers coming inside the Lusty Lady just for a break. I'm glad I chanted a lot this morning, I find myself thinking about Scott, our lifestyles are very different, don't know that it could be a "serious" type relationship but I feel so comfortable with him even when avoiding the issue.

I hope I don't dread every workday like this. Always wishing I didn't have to work in this kind of sexual industry. Wow. Prostitution would kill me.

February 19.

Last night wasn't too bad. They came to see us, not the parade. Although we did have the parade crowd, that giggled and disappeared very quickly. Some guys, a threesome, I danced for them. They just wanted to see between my legs. They held up two fingers. It looked like the "peace" sign. So I held up two fingers and said, "Peace." It was my best line yet. Anyway they got rude but I couldn't hear them. Security tossed them out and Martin came around the other side to say I didn't have to put up with verbal abuse. I honestly didn't know what they were saying. But it made me feel good that security was looking out for me. Martin walked me to the bus stop, he was very distant, not in the least intimate. Not ever giving eye contact. I guess that's how he does his job. He has a great Australian, I think, accent.

NSA (*Nichiren Shoshu* of America) people stare when they find out I'm dancing. Larry really made me mad today. I went to him about activities while we were all hurry- up-and-waiting for a picture taking. I needed to give instructions to one of the newer members and Larry looked at me in the most annoyed fashion. Like I was a pest. Tae noticed it. Okay, I still call Larry occasionally because he was my best friend for a long time and sometimes I think of something that I want to tell him, or sometimes I'm just plain lonely. Or think of something we have in common. You can't just shut off almost two years of your life and wipe out the history you share. There's so much in me, likes and dislikes, things that happened, stories that happened in those years.

Picaro would be a cool place to shoot a café scene in a film. The Roxie outside the front window looks really neat and there's several proscenium one could use. Screens to wall off the back seating section and use that for cameras, dressing, etc. and set up the front as a café. There's a ceiling fan and everything. There's a window at the divider between front and back that could be used.

February 20, Monday

I had fun at work today. I was really energized and developing new moves. One customer stayed all day to see me. Looked like my Uncle Lynn. Maybe it was, but I don't think so. I think I'd really have fun if I got a wig, changed my name, and really developed a stage character. Hello Inertia Rhapsody.

I just played cards with this guy, we were having fun. I think he was trying to pick up on me. Then I gestured to him and he flew out of there so fast which was great cuz I was trying to figure out how to get rid of him. I got weird vibes from him.

February 25, Saturday.

So I have a "paramour" Scott Damon Morris, very fun. Last Tuesday night I called him, and said "I'm bored, let's do something free..."

He came over immediately. We went for a walk up to the Castro, Eureka Park where we kissed passionately. Then came back here where we were together.

I was nervous. It's been two years that the only man I've been with was Larry and it's been months since I've had sex at all. Scott was easy to be with, to talk to but doesn't like to be called a boyfriend. That's why I called him my paramour.

At work there was a customer snorting coke. I called him on it. Say "No."

Before work I was at a Buddhist meeting and chanted to get home safely which I did. Another dancer was going to Bartlett and 25th so I shared her cab. And I worked again Thursday A.M. Managed to be fairly awake for that. Later I felt sexually needy and called Scott again.

He said, "Do you believe in love?"

"Yes. What is it to you?"

"It's inside you," he said. "And as you open to a person it begins to envelope that person, then goes back and as the relationship grows the love grows and comes out more and more. Retreating less and less. Enveloping the one you love."

Later, I do remember he said, "What am I writing on your back?"

"L?" Yes. "I?" No. "L...O...V...and a backwards E."

Awfully sentimental coming from a non-conventional, non-monogamist, socialist, messenger. And throughout Thursday night our coupling became less frantic. We slept well next to each other, and I began to feel that love coming out of me more and more.

Although this love is on a retreat at the moment.   It's Saturday night and I haven't seen or heard from him since he left for work Friday morning, which is no big deal.

One thing he said to me was just because I don't call for four days doesn't mean I like you less, or don't want to be with you. It would be nice to know he's thinking about me as I'm thinking about him. Oh I'm remembering bits of his speech on Love.

It's when you see a sunset and wish they were with you to share it. Etc. Kind of like a Hallmark card. But sincere. If not, he's a good actor.

So Friday I crashed. I'd slept weird, if at all, all week. I slept till afternoon when Ana called, fortunately or I'd have missed our lunch date. So I had lunch then ice cream with Ana.

Went to Barbara's to chant and William talked to me. He's warmed up to me. So then I walked home. Walking down Haight, this shitzy guy just walks up and starts talking really stupid. I chanted inside for him to go away. To get rid of him nicely, walking by Ground Zero, I looked in and there was [my Buddhist friend,] Ron Stone, sitting there with a woman. I hated to interrupt but I had to drop this shitzy guy so I said, "There's a friend I need to talk to." And I ducked in. Told Ron the experience and he said, "Chanting does work." So we talked. After they left I thought about my *internam dainmoku* and how it had really been working lately. I just wish it would affect my finances.

Passion

AJB: March 12, 1989
It is New Orleans in July.
My body damp, and
Heavy with the humidity.
You are a tall glass of ice tea.
You are the Gulf of Mexico.

My hair, clinging to my neck in strands,
My skin tastes like the rim of a margarita glass, you lick.
You are a tall glass of ice tea with a mint leaf in it.
You are the Gulf of Mexico.

Friday

I've worked every day this week –lots of hours. My neck hurts. *Gongyo*'s been bad -- missed a couple days all together. I have some sort of infection, probably a yeast infection, and Scott's enthusiasm has waned substantially. While I was "with him" it was amazing but it feels gone. I'm not going to overreact. Could be a stage. I just want to be with someone who likes being around me, and we've never even spent a day together.

At the *Lusty Lady* there was a customer I called Marty – he looks like a Marty. I think that his name's Dave. He is such a nerd and he acts like he thinks he's such the swinger. Maybe he is, or maybe he imagines he is. He hangs out forever. I think he's endearing cuz he's such a nerd and he doesn't have an arrogant attitude and he's having fun.

On Wednesday, a real obnoxious young man came in. Motioned for me to come to him. I said only if you say, "Please." As we don't give special attention on demand. I was being friendly though. Then he said in a real abusive loud vice. "I want to fxxx you." I told him we don't dance for abusive people. I actually felt at a loss. I didn't know what to say. I wanted to be tough but didn't know how. So I just said, "That wasn't a nice thing to say." Real wimpy like and walked away. But none of the dancers danced for him and we finally ordered him out. Lots of that this week. I guess cuz I'm working every day, I'm noticing the jerks and standing up for myself. But today though I was totally out of energy. Not into moving at all.

I've been offered part time work at Diner – Allied. Filing 4 hours a day. I hate filing. But I just want to get into Diner. I'll have to talk to them. It only pays $5.70 per hour but I think I'll take it. It's a straight job steady work and hopefully I'll get a discount on film processing. Could be especially lucrative when I go back to school.

March 6, Monday.

So Scott is a boring-no-good-jerk. There. That's all there is to it. If he calls I'll tell him he missed his chance, but I don't have time for someone who cares so little for me. If he doth protest, I'll just say "Prove it." I need attention. Not a monopoly on time just a certain degree of attention, a picnic in the park, a trip on the coast, a hike, a movie, an afternoon in mutual silence reading and writing in a cafe' with sporadic exchange of ideas. Not an everyday obsessive relationship. A friend and lover. Not a weekly sexual encounter. There's a chance he will never call me again.

There's a chance he'll call and we'll agree its basically a done deal. Perhaps with intentions of a future friendship that will never really happen. But if it were a movie I'd say "I don't have the time to waste my energy on this kind of friendship.

In the café

<u>March 10, Friday.</u>
There's a character. She has orange hair and a black dress with orange skull and cross bones in the pattern all over it. Punk is being manufactured, that's old news even, but I guess the really gross thing is that the pattern is so pattern-like and in neat straight lines of skull and cross bones. That's the kind of detail that exposes you as a "poser."
So Scott called where I left off above. I kind of wimped out, not totally though. I talked about how I needed more attention but wasn't looking for a monopoly on his time. He talked about how he doesn't like being around people when he's out of it. Sometimes he gets intensely weird and awful to be around. So I played it cool and put him off a few more days. (I'm getting it together first.) I feel neglected 'cause he didn't call for days and I say without bitching, just stating that emotionally I need more attention. Then I put him off for a few more days focusing on the weekend. I want to go on a picnic. I've never played these games before. It's kind of fun. He says. "You're insatiable." Hum.   So Wednesday night I called and left a message. I went to a double feature. Presumably he didn't get the message but anyway, I saw Mae West (the original Lusty Lady) in *I'm No Angel* and *The Blonde Bombshell.*
Last night I saw the *Queen of Swords* on T.V. which was great. It inspired me to invite Scott over, which is kind of funny really.
He was very enthusiastic about sleeping next to me but not interested in having sex at all.

<u>March 12, Sunday.</u>
Fumiko ground me into the ground. "The three poisons are greed, anger, and stupidity. To understand life we need only look inside as we have all existences inside us. We have the ten worlds

and each world has ten worlds, so we have three-thousand life potentials within us. That is *ichinen sanzen*; but to tap them we must have a strong life condition. You cannot have a strong life condition without practicing dynamically."

I want to go to school but I can't even get it together to fill out the application and I think I'm strong enough to work these principles. Heck, Fumiko had just tumbled down the world I made for myself so neatly. So I have to quit the exotic dancing and "How will I survive?"

Who will be my friend?

Scott will probably go with the deal. Do I even care. I want someone who'll take me on a picnic. Scott will never take me on a picnic. Not while I'm at the *Lusty Lady*. While I'm there I'll be treated as a Lusty Lady. I need a friend.

Sour milk culture grown in preparation for Mexico.
April one, the carton say,
 As it oozed with a plop to my cup.
 April Fools.
 Sorry Hon, if that was a special project
         to go with your cheese,
It's down the sink, won't set your trip back. I hope.

My name is _____ - I've been chanting one year and four months.

When I started chanting I had terrible housing Karma. When I first moved into the city I lived in a string of unlivable places with negative environments and drug dealers, to tiny cold rooms, to potheads who were too spaced out to be responsible room-mates. My first big benefit was a new place to live where I had only one room-mate and the room to have privacy and do my art work, with common space as well.

This benefit was challenged in September of last fall; along with many other things in my life. I was unemployed looking for a job to advance my life. I was having trouble with my boyfriend, we were in the process of breaking up. Then my room-mate, giving me 2 days notice, left town. He took the T.V. set, his parrot, his phone answering machine. He left me with two months back rent to pay, a lease in his name, a $250 PG&E bill, and a house full of his junk. The table and couch and chairs were appreciated, the closets full of old photographs, fishing gear, papers, old clothes were overwhelming. I spent the first week hiding – spending as little time at home as possible. The next week I wrote the landlord with a proposed arrangement to pay off the rent and obtain the lease over time, and I began to slowly clean indiscriminately throwing away my room-mate's past.

Not having a job stretched my finances to the limit and I began looking like a potato but it gave me time enough to clean the house which took weeks to do.

October one came and I had to have a room-mate. I had advertised at Rainbow Grocery and a few other places but had no luck, on the first a woman called, Mary. She came over and we talked a while and seemed to get along. I didn't have time to really screen her. At first she seemed really neat, but almost immediately her behavior became really erratic. I was working two jobs and never knew if the house was going to be rearranged by the time I got home.

On Saturday I met with the landlord and his partner. The roommate told the landlord I was irresponsible and not to be trusted. I was confused and didn't know how to proceed. She made me cry in front of the landlord. I thought I would loose my place. Finally I gained control, ignored her, and tried my best to just talk to the landlord. She screamed at me the whole time.

I chanted and knew then that she had a serious speed problem, as much as she denied it.

That night I wrote a note. …

May 4, Thursday.
I have one day left at Diner Allied.

Today I ran across the street and onto the #15 bus, Kearney. I rode it up Kearney past where Columbus begins, the stop I used to get off at to go to the Lusty Lady. I used to fantasize about staying on the bus and riding on to go to work at Omega Productions. Which is what I did today.

On the way home today I saw a small cluster of well-dressed attitudes. The leading attitude is a man suit, with white hair balding and a white beard. He was raising his arm to signal for a cab. As if he were conducting an orchestra. The Veteran's Cab was not musical, being occupied, but the Yellow Cab accepted the part.

I am not sad to leave the Diner. Working three jobs is exhausting. I really like Omega and Underwater Resources both.

I am missing Larry again.

Appendix Two
A Child's Story

Muncho the Mouse

by Allyson Bennett, 1975   Rewrite by Celeste Rose 2005

One day Muncho the mouse took his canvas shopping bag and went to the health-food store to buy grains, nuts, and dried berries. At the check-out counter was a sign advertising a cruise. *Write your name here and drop it in this jar.* So he did.

Weeks later Mother Mouse answered the phone. "This is the Food Barn. We have good news for Muncho, he has won a cruise on a nice little boat called The Lollipop."

Mother Mouse made him a sailor suit, blue and white with a square collar. Father Mouse bought him a sailor hat. They packed his little mouse-sized suitcase with a towel, swimsuit, Hawaiian shirt, sunscreen and sunglasses.

It was early in December when Muncho walked down to the bay. He walked on the long wooden wharf carrying his suitcase and proudly wearing his sailor suit and hat.

He passed a super-sized boat with smoke stacks that reached to the sky...that wasn't it. He past a yacht with brass railings and a lady wearing diamond rings and fancy clothes....that wasn't it. At the end of the wharf, there was a very small sailboat, all painted bright colors. A gangplank flopped over the water. The name painted on the bow was "The Lollipop." Muncho looked at his ticket...this was it!

The small cruise boat sailed out into the peaceful ocean. Muncho watched the sails catch the wind. The captain who was a duck stood at the helm guiding the boat toward the south. The seven little sailors were seven little white mice.

All was well until the middle of the night. Muncho woke up. Oooo, his stomach was hungry. So he got out of bed and climbed up the ladder to see what he could find.

The boat rocked in the gentle breeze. The water sparkled in the moonlight.

Then Muncho noticed that the boat-rescue-rings tied along the railings were different colors...cherry red, lime green, lemon yellow. He sniffed. "Yum." They were candy lifesavers! So he ate all the lifesavers along the port side of the boat and all the lifesavers along the starboard side of the boat. He sat back in the moonlight to enjoy the full feeling in his tummy when he noticed that the main mast had red and white stripes all the way up to the top...It was a giant candy cane.

So Muncho ate it and "oops" the sail came tumbling down. He fell with his little pink nose right on the boards. The deck was dark brown, sweet smelling and shiny...It was made of chocolate! He took a small bite and it was so tasty that he ate the whole thing. Then Muncho ate the hull of the boat, which was made of gingerbread. Suddenly the ocean water came pouring into the boat and The Lollipop began to sink.

Captain Duck, yelled in his loud quacking voice. "Abandon ship, everyone into the life boat!"

"Ay ay, sir." said the seven little white mice and they rowed away with the captain swimming along beside, shouting, "Quack, quack." But they left Muncho behind.

"What about me?" Muncho shouted.

As The Lollipop filled with water and drifted down, down, down, Muncho floated out into the lonely ocean. Swimming dog paddle, he hoped that one of the life boats would come back and save him. He was happy when he found a piece of flotsam and climbed on top. Then he noticed that it was two marshmallows with a piece of graham cracker on top. "Yum, Smores!" So he ate the little raft on which he sat and landed in the water. "Splash."

"Help, help, please someone save me." He dog paddled in the water. His mouth opened and shut as he hollered for help. Then he tasted the water. It wasn't salty. It was sweet and sour...the ocean was made of lemonade.

Muncho drank the sea and paddled. Pretty soon he came to an island and it was a soggy mouse that collapsed on the sand but very grateful to be out of the ocean, even if it was lemonade. After a while, he was hungry again so he walked around the island. There was nothing but sand--no coconut trees, no dates, no raisins. He ended up back where he started and fell on his face, kicking his feet, banging with his fists and yelling. "I'm hungry, I'm tired, I want my Mama."

His face fell into the sand. His mouth popped open. "I want my Mama." He got sand all in his mouth. But..."Yum yum." It wasn't sand. Muncho had landed on a place called Sugar Island, the sand was made of sugar. Then Muncho ate, by the finger full and by the fist full, all the sugar he ever wanted.

Two years later. The Tootsie-Roll-Helicopter-Weather-Watch-Company was flying over the Lemonade Sea looking for cotton candy clouds and lemon tasting raindrops, when John, the second pilot said, "I don't see Sugar Island."

Sally, the first pilot, said, "Maybe we're in the wrong place....Wait a minute...I see something."

When the helicopter hovered down, there was Sugar Island but it was now tiny and there was a great big mouse lying on the beach. He had a smile on his face.

John radioed, "Bay tower from Tootsie Roll. About that lost mouse? Well I think Sally and I might have found him. Ha ha, I think that mouse nearly ate all of Sugar Island. Over."

Muncho's mother was happy to have her Muncho home again. She fixed a big supper of vegetables and cheese. The she gave him a kiss and a big slice of white cake with lemon frosting. "No thank you, Mama," said Muncho, pushing the plate away. "I've had plenty of sugar. Could I have seconds on broccoli?"

The End

Made in the USA
Charleston, SC
24 October 2012